THE WITCHES' WISDOM TAROT GUIDEBOOK

PHYLLIS CUROTT

ARTWORK BY

DANIELLE BARLOW

HAY HOUSE

Carlsbad, California • New York City
London • Sydney • New Delhi

Published in the United Kingdom by:
Hay House UK Ltd, The Sixth Floor, Watson House
54 Baker Street, London W1U 7BU
Tel: +44 (0)20 3927 7290; www.hayhouse.co.uk

Published in the United States of America by:
Hay House Inc., PO Box 5100, Carlsbad, CA 92018-5100
Tel: (1) 760 431 7695 or (800) 654 5126; www.hayhouse.com

Published in Australia by:
Hay House Australia Ltd, 18/36 Ralph St, Alexandria NSW 2015
Tel: (61) 2 9669 4299; www.hayhouse.com.au

Published in India by:
Hay House Publishers India, Muskaan Complex, Plot No.3, B-2,
Vasant Kunj, New Delhi 110 070
Tel: (91) 11 4176 1620; www.hayhouse.co.in

A catalogue record for this book is available from the British Library.

ISBN: 978-1-78817-995-9

Printed and bound in China by Imago Group

FSC
www.fsc.org
MIX
Paper | Supporting responsible forestry
FSC® C005748

Contents

INTERPRETATIONS OF THE CARDS

THE MINOR ARCANA

AIR

FIRE

⟅ Earth ⟆

⟅ The Major Arcana ⟆

Introduction

Working with any Tarot opens a world of wonder and possibility. The Witches' Wisdom Tarot opens a world of wonder and wisdom, possibility and magic. And you don't have to be a Witch to benefit from Witches' wisdom.

Witches have always seen into the heart of the Sacred, into people's hearts, and into the future. As a Witch, I know that power of seeing. In fact, I'm a Witch because of what a Witch saw in my first Tarot reading 40 years ago.

As a young woman living in New York City, I thought my vision of the ordinary world gave me all the insights and empowerment I needed. I was a social justice lawyer fighting organized crime in trade unions, struggling to make the world a better place. But my ordinary life was starting to fill with magical occurrences for which I had no logical explanation—dreams came true and impossible intuitions were accurate; synchronicities, signs, and sensitivities were expanding my perception.

And then one day, at the urging of a friend, I found myself in the back of a dusty, dimly lit bookstore, seated across a tiny table from a plump, dark-haired woman busily shuffling a deck of oversized Tarot cards.

Strange as it was, I felt utterly calm, willing, ready. For the next hour she told me about my life, but what impressed me most was when she described a secret that I had shared with no one.

As she gathered up the cards, she asked me the question that changed my life: "I have a women's circle that meets every week. I think you might find what you're looking for there. Why don't you come?"

I thanked her politely, said I'd think about it, paid her, and left. I didn't think about it. After all, she was a *Witch*.

I got on with my life, months passed, and then one afternoon a woman who had repeatedly appeared in my dreams appeared before me at the Metropolitan Museum of Art. She was larger than life and carved from marble. The plaque beside her said: "The Libyan Sibyl." *Sibyl* means "Witch."

For the next three and a half years, I studied with a hidden coven of Witches and my life filled with magic.

Despite 500 years of defamation and persecution, today Witchcraft is the fastest growing form of spirituality in the United States and is spreading across the globe. And the world needs its Witches more than ever. Witches have always known how to live in a sacred way, because they live in a sacred world. Witches know that Spirit and Earth are One.

Though much has been lost, we have the same techniques as the Witches of old, and the same great spiritual teacher, Nature. We remember what Witches have always known: that magic happens when we open our hearts and invite Spirit to flow into us and through us into the world. Spells, rituals, practices, and techniques are how we work with that divine energy, giving it form and shape in our lives and in the world.

Magic is an essential part of who we are. But sometimes we doubt ourselves. We doubt that magic is real. We doubt that the world is charged through with divinity. We need a mirror to see clearly, a spell to clear the way, a guide to help us find our way.

We need divination, Witch or not. Divination is magic in action. And one of the best divination tools is the Tarot.

After a long apprenticeship with Mother Earth, I was thrilled when Michelle Pilley, publisher and managing director of Hay House UK, invited me to create a new Witches' Tarot. Magic was afoot from the very start and shortly thereafter a series of synchronicities in Michelle's life brought the perfect artist, Danielle Barlow, into the project.

Although at first glance we seem quite different, Danielle and I knew we were meant to work together. She describes herself as "private and reserved," but she's incredibly present, open, and active in her community. For some 20 years she's been a practicing Hedgewitch, someone whose work is deeply rooted in the physical and Spirit realms of the natural world, the plants, wild creatures, rocks, and rivers where she lives. She's also a gifted painter, published illustrator, and the creator of the numinous *The Green Wheel Oracle*. Danielle is also a sought-after incense maker, a trained horticulturalist, a very busy mother of three, and a caretaker of animals and land. She lives, creates, and makes Earth-based magic on the northern edge of the wild moorland, bogs, and granite tors of Dartmoor in the southwest of England. Remarkably, she'd only ever had one Tarot reading, right before we began working together.

I'm one of America's first public Witches, though by nature I'm quite private and contemplative. Shortly after my neo-Gardnerian initiation 40 years ago, I was the first to merge contemporary Witchcraft with core shamanism, gradually creating my own tradition of shamanic Wicca, the Temple of Ara, which is devoted to the universal spiritual wisdom of Mother Earth and has grown into an international community.

I'm also an attorney and activist who's fought for the rights of Witches, women, and Mother Earth; the author of four internationally bestselling books; and a teacher who is helping make Witchcraft accessible to the world. Single and without children, I've spent much of my life in New York City and "on the road." Now I live out in farm country and spend a great deal of time with the Ara community in Italy. I've read Tarot cards for as long as I've been a Witch.

Danielle's a very grounded Virgo, I'm a very philosophical Aquarius, and our differences turned out to be blessings, but we're more similar than different. We're both devoted to a shamanic approach to practicing Witchcraft, to the embodied divinity and spiritual wisdom of Mother Earth, to the accessibility of Spirit realms and guidance of Spirit beings, and to working with the *genius loci* or Spirits of place. Together, we walk a healing path home to a sacred planet.

Our connection began before meeting: without knowing what the other was doing, we both used journeying, an ancient shamanic technique for gaining guidance and insight, to seek answers to the same question: "What do we need to know to create a new Witches' Tarot?"

When we spoke, we discovered we'd been given the same answer: "Begin with the elements—Air, Fire, Water, and Earth—not their symbols. Ask them what the world needs to know and they will show you."

We agreed that we would use journeying to create a new Witches' Tarot that would be meaningful, magical, and rich with wisdom for Witches and for the world. Journeying has been used by Indigenous peoples across the globe for thousands of years. It's a "spiritual technology" that "hacks" the brain with steady percussive drumming (or rattling) to open consciousness and perception. This altered state gives the journeyer access to Spirit realms to work with power animals and Spirit guides, allies and teachers, and return to this world with healing, wisdom, and other blessings, including the ability to see the Sacred. It's an amazingly effective technique in which Danielle and I were already skilled and which we were confident was the method for discovering our deck.

Given its common ground with modern Witchcraft and its proven efficacy and popularity, we decided to follow the path laid out by the Rider Tarot Deck, starting, as we had been instructed, with the elements—the four suits of the Minor Arcana. We would proceed in the order in which a Witches' circle is cast in the Northern Hemisphere, starting with Air in the East, then Fire in the South, Water in the West, and Earth in the North. We would journey together into all 56 cards of the Minor Arcana, a combined total of at least 112 journeys, then into the 22 mysteries of the Major Arcana, which brought the total to 156 journeys (with more for clarification).

As a Tarot reader, I didn't want to overthink or anticipate the meanings of the cards based on what I already knew. We both wanted them to speak for themselves, to show us what we, and the world, *didn't* know and *needed* to know.

We took about a year to journey, discuss, discern, decide, draw, paint, write, edit, utilize, revise, and submit, while continuing to journey and discuss throughout. It was an epic quest. Along the way, we often had similar experiences, images, and teachings, or found that when we put our different journeys together, a fuller meaning was revealed.

Together, we chose the images that captured the essence of what we were shown. Images from my journeys are in Danielle's beautiful illustrations, and language from hers is in my vision-provoking text. It's been an extraordinarily creative and magical partnership and friendship, a challenging and life-changing adventure. And we have been accompanied every step of the way by wise guides and compassionate teachers. They are waiting to accompany you, too, as you use Witches' wisdom to awaken magic in your life.

Witches' Wisdom

The roots of Witches' wisdom are more than 5,000 years old. A *wicce*, the original spelling, was a wise one, a seer, a shaman, and healer of our Indigenous Ancestors. Witches traveled into realms of Spirit and returned to this world with blessings for their communities. They have always known the healing power of plants and places of power, the wisdom of animals and the Earth itself. They know the wild and divine magic of Nature, and they know the wildness and divinity of human nature. Witches know the world is full of magic because it's full of divinity.

Witches have always known, too, that the world of Spirit is accessible and that the Earthly plane is fully divine. Moving beyond the limits of time and space and into realms of Spirit, they return with gifts, including the gift of sight—

into the hearts of those who need help, into the future, and into the divinity and magic of this realm. Witches know that Spirit and Nature and humanity are One. That's the source of their wisdom and magic. That's the vision animating the Witches' Wisdom Tarot.

Tarot—Meaning and Magic

The Witches' Wisdom Tarot is full of magic. To fully manifest that magic, it's useful to know about three crucial events in the history of Tarot. The Tarot (*tarocchi*) appeared in Italy in the 14th century, just as Witches were disappearing. The 78 unnamed and unnumbered cards of the deck were divided into two categories: 22 "trumps" with mysterious figures; and 56 cards, organized in four "suits" or "pips" — spades/Swords, hearts/Cups, clubs/Wands, and diamonds/Coins. Originally used for gaming and gambling, the cards were quickly put to the task of foretelling the future, primarily by and for women.

Then, beginning in the late 18th century, theories about the Tarot's mystical origins and purpose began to appear. None were ever corroborated, but its reinvention as an esoteric path for spiritual awakening had begun. The trumps were renamed the Major Arcana and the suits the Minor Arcana, activating the cards' potency and possibilities—*arcana* means "mysterious or specialized knowledge, language, or information only accessible to or possessed by an initiate."

In 1910, artist Pamela Colman Smith and writer Arthur Waite, two initiates of the Hermetic Order of the Golden Dawn, a British esoteric group, created a Tarot deck that revolutionized the appearance, meaning, and use of the Tarot. The Golden Dawn was devoted to the alchemical refinement of the human Spirit and its members practiced ceremonial magic in order to change consciousness at will, transforming the lead of an unknowing mind into the gold of an enlightened Spirit. Their Tarot deck, published by the Rider company (so, for brevity, the Rider deck), was a guide to the soul's journey.

Smith replaced the Minor Arcana's geometric arrangement of symbols with human figures engaged in a wide range of the daily activities, events, and emotions that make up the journey of human life. She used the Golden Dawn's system of magical correspondences, which drew on the work of early Greek philosophers, to help tell these stories, incorporating the elements and their symbols or magical tools—Air/Swords, Fire/Wands, Water/Cups and Earth/Pentacles (Coins)—as metaphors for the journey of human life.

The second half of the revolution was the new interpretation provided by Waite, particularly with regard to the Major Arcana, which he also numbered and named. He focused on correspondences between the Tarot, esoteric magic, and the Qabbalah (a body of Jewish mysticism) to craft new meanings for the cards. He also included simple fortune-telling formulas like: "Perfect contentment, felicity, ecstasy; also speedy intelligence; gold," but his most significant contribution was the use of the Major Arcana as a meditative and magical map for the soul's transformation. That has been its purpose and value for esoteric practitioners ever since. (The Minors were considered of less importance for this purpose.)

Soon, other knowledge systems like numerology and astrology were integrated into Tarot interpretation, and the Tarot became a tapestry connecting Western mystical systems. The esoteric philosophy, practice, and symbols of the Golden Dawn that were integrated into the Rider deck also had an important influence on the modern revival of Witchcraft. An example is the Table of Correspondences, which organizes the four elements and their related magical tools, along with aspects of Nature and human nature, deities, and more.

The next important shift occurred in the 1980s, when a group of Tarot writers and readers, primarily women, took Tarot interpretation in a modern direction. Expanding on their knowledge of the esoteric interpretation, Rachel Pollock, Mary Greer, Angeles Arrien, Gail Fairfield, James Wanless, and others reinterpreted the cards using a new system of knowledge—psychology.

Psychologist Carl Jung's conception of archetypes, powerful universal energies or patterns in humanity's individual and collective unconscious, now explained why the Major Arcana held such potent psychological meaning for seekers, and his theories of synchronicity (meaningful coincidences generated by the deep consciousness of the person experiencing them) explained how the Tarot cards worked with such remarkable accuracy. The Minor Arcana cards, with their depictions of daily life, took on a deeper value than they had for esotericists and "fortune-tellers." Tarot became an increasingly popular tool to help people understand themselves better and so transform their lives.

The trend ever since has been toward this more "humanistic" Tarot. This approach integrates the Rider deck's esoteric symbolism and dynamics with the insights of psychology to explain the influences that affect and motivate us and make us who we are. The advice of the Delphic Oracle—"Know thyself"—reverberates in today's interpretation: self-awareness, personal growth, *and* the possibility of awakening to the presence of a living, conscious, and caring Universe. There is an essential harmony of purpose to both approaches—giving people greater insight into themselves *and* their innate capacities to create lives of meaning and fulfillment within a greater, even divine, context.

Rider Tarot cards are rich with symbolism, and one no longer has to be an initiate to understand the code or a psychologist to apply Jungian interpretations. And with the Minor Arcana's remarkable accuracy in foretelling, the Rider deck has long been the gold standard (alchemical pun intended) in the creation of countless new decks. Its influence has meant the Tarot's imagery, interpretations, and values have remained largely unaltered for the last 100 years, though the human figures have been increasingly replaced by a variety of characters, from cats to comic book heroes. Even modern Witches' decks still rely heavily on the Rider deck's imagery.

Today, the Tarot has become a mirror in which to see the hidden and holy self within, a telescope to see what lies ahead, *and* a method of magical/spiritual transformation. But we continue to search for deeper self-awareness, greater foresight, and more meaningful magic. Why? Because something essential is missing from the Rider deck and its progeny. As Rachel Pollock wisely noted, "... any system of divination will tell us something, but the quality of that something depends on the values within the system."

The Rider deck is popular because it's incredibly useful for self-knowledge and for predicting the future, which is what most seekers want from the Tarot. But, like fish that don't know they're swimming in Water, it's very important, *especially* for Witches, to understand the deck's *values*, as these color the advice it gives.

The Rider deck was radical in its day, but was still heavily influenced by Abrahamic theology and thinking. You see it in the extensive use of biblical imagery like crucifixes, churches, angels, the Hierophant, Devil, Chariot, and Judgment. The Rider deck presents a spiritual journey ascending from the mundane preoccupations of daily life on the Earthly plane to the heavenly realms of pure consciousness, energy, and transcendent Spirit. The seeker's journey always rises *away* from the material world, which is perfectly illustrated by the unintentionally ironic image of the final Major Arcana card, The World, XXI, which depicts a floating figure suspended in space surrounded by the symbols of four archangels. Enlightenment means leaving the Earth behind. *That* is the value system at the heart of the Rider deck.

What's missing is Witches' wisdom.

The Witches' Wisdom Tarot

The Minor Arcana

Air, my breath,
Fire, my Spirit,
Water, my blood,
and Earth, my body.

This was one of the first Witches' chants I learned many years ago. For Witches and others, including Tarot readers, working with the elements has been a powerful way of deepening self-awareness:

- ***Air*** corresponds to the gifts of the human mind, like intelligence and intuition, language and communication.
- ***Fire*** corresponds to our willpower, courage, passion, and determination.
- ***Water*** corresponds to our emotions, to the heart, love, and dreams.
- ***Earth*** corresponds to our work, material possessions, wealth, and creativity.

When Danielle and I asked the elements what we needed to know, the deck's guides and teachers appeared: Fox, Grandmother Toad, Briar Rose, and Mycelium. They, along with other Spirits, allies, and guides, led us into a world of wisdom, wildness, wonder, revelation, and raw magic. We flew on the wind between the stars, greeted the rising Sun at dawn, dove deep into grief and beauty with singing whales, and grew in wild, chaotic, and green profusion.

We were quickly shown that the elements weren't human symbols or metaphors, but potent forces of Nature with their own intrinsic value, purpose, and consciousness. We were shown the self-awareness of Nature.

As we journeyed, the elements and their Animal and Plant Peoples and Spirit forms revealed a world of beauty, complexity, and divinity, a world that encompasses our humanity and stretches far beyond our conscious limits. Yet we've spent thousands of years separating ourselves from Nature, believing that our human consciousness makes us superior to it and entitled to have power and control over it. The result has been a hole in our hearts, our Spirits, and our lives, and a deep wounding of Mother Earth and a diminishing of her ability to sustain life.

When you first look at the Minor Arcana cards of the Witches' Wisdom Tarot, you may even feel that you've entered an alien world—that's how cut off from Nature we've become.

The only humans in the Minor Arcana are the Shapeshifters, formerly the Court Cards, who are bridges connecting us with Spirit *and* Nature. But as you work with the imagery of the cards and the guidance of the text, with the plants and animals and all the wonders of Nature, you'll see their beauty, experience their reality, and gain a new understanding of Life. You'll feel their magic working.

The elements want us to remember that they are part of us, just as we are part of Nature. They offer us a healing path to wholeness. Each card is a revelation of missing wisdom about Nature and Spirit and some missing, natural, and divine part of ourselves. The Minor Arcana offer paths to unknown parts of ourselves and to an awareness beyond ourselves—an awareness of ourselves as part of a greater, interdependent, divine whole.

And they had important new lessons for us about their true nature, and ours. Air revealed the *purpose* of consciousness: awareness of the unifying presence and power of *divine Love*. Fire wanted us to understand that *because* it's the spark of life, its greatest power is *joy*. Water showed us that it's a *messenger*, carrying everything put into it throughout Creation. It also revealed how embodied our emotions are and should be. Earth revealed that, in addition to its countless blessings of manifestation that nourish body and soul, it's the element of *healing*.

Air and Fire, Water and Earth all challenged the way we humans, and Witches in particular, think about and interact with Nature. Immediately, the element of Air, which the Rider deck depicts with a lot of negative imagery about the human mind's neuroses, showed us the magic of changing consciousness at will—from negative to positive, revealing right ways of thinking rather than depicting the wrong ways. And the context was always *Love*.

Like Nature itself, some imagery, particularly that of the "5" card of each element, did depict challenges, dire consequences, or dangers, but along with those challenges, choices were always offered. The elemental energies consistently revealed themselves as life-sustaining powers of love, joy, support, and healing. And that made perfect sense, since we knew at the heart of the Witches' Wisdom Tarot was the unity of Spirit and Creation, of energy and embodiment.

We began to see and experience new magic. The Minor Arcana shared important new ways of approaching and working with the elements when we made magic. They asked us to stop "using" them for selfish purposes and showed us how to *work with them* for our wellbeing *and* for purposes greater than our own, for the Great Magic of Creation.

For example, what we put into Water is shared with everything. That challenges the way Witches traditionally "use" Water to clean away negativity, pain, and suffering, the way everyone uses Water for cleaning away waste. Instead of putting our garbage into Water to be taken away, we were told to bring Water's purity into ourselves. That purity transforms us positively from within and is a blessing to be received with gratitude. Then, what leaves us and enters Water can be recycled and put to good use by Nature. Self-care and care of Nature are in harmony. Naturally, it works.

Nature truly is our great spiritual teacher. After more than 120 journeys to learn from the elements, we found not only were we changed, but so was our appreciation of the world we returned to—it was charged with divinity. We could hear the Earth's voice and see the Earth's blessings in the land, sea, and star-filled sky, and in all the beings residing with us on the planet. It was humbling and empowering.

It was also heartbreaking to witness the life-threatening damage we humans have done and the future that damage portends. We had to struggle with overwhelming feelings of grief, powerlessness, and responsibility. But the wisdom we received and have shared in the Witches' Wisdom Tarot is healing, inspiring, and empowering, and can help us create the future we want and need—the future all living things deserve.

Everything we need to remedy the damage we've done and to heal ourselves and our planet is around and within us. Air, Fire, Water, and Earth showed us how to contend with the challenges of life and how to receive the love, joy, connection, and abundance that are natural to life.

So, the Minor Arcana reveal our natural, whole, and holy selves and guide us in recovering our wild and wise essence as part of Nature and as an embodiment of Spirit. They reveal the future as it could and should be, *and* how to create it.

These are some of the gifts given to us by the elements that we share in the Witches Wisdom Tarot.

Prepared for the next part of our journey, we entered the realm of the Major Arcana.

The Major Arcana

The Major Arcana are cards of destiny. When they appear, we sense that something insistent, life-changing, and sacred is summoning us. We *know* magic is happening.

Are these images spiritual beings or archetypes, real people, deities, or entities? *Yes*—all of them and mysteriously more. Like holy fountains carrying boulders and gold, they erupt from deep within and come from realms of Spirit to disrupt our plans, challenge our expectations, and push us past our limitations. They are the energies that catalyze our lives and galvanize our inner divinity. When the Divine speaks to us through the Tarot, the Major Arcana are the messengers who command our attention.

How would they appear to two Witches?

We again set off on the well-traveled path of the Rider deck, named and ordered by Waite, with its sequence from 0, the innocent Fool, to XXI, the wise World. For generations of Tarot readers, it's offered a guide to self-awareness and enlightenment that ascends from the physical to the spiritual, away from the Earth and the body to heaven and otherworldliness. It was not necessarily the way a Witch's compass would point, but what other way was there?

Our first journey was a shock.

We found ourselves in the World and it was on Fire. As we watched, a young woman in hiking boots with a heavy pack on her back strode away from a burning metropolis and into a natural landscape. We had entered the World as it is at this very moment—civilized and self-destructing, yet still wildly natural and beautifully wise. We had met the Pilgrim, and she was nobody's Fool. For the next 21 days, we traveled with her.

Our next journeys found her in circumstances very different from the Judgment card in the Rider Deck, XX, with its Christian imagery of figures rising from their graves at the summoning of a heavenly angel. The Pilgrim had paused by a clear and flowing stream to rest, reflect, and drink, as two young foxes shredded her burdens and a wily badger carried off a piece of her past.

The Major Arcana had reversed direction.

When the Pilgrim was ready, we moved on to the Luminaries—the Sun, XIX now 3; Moon, XVIII now 4; and Star, XVII now 5—and down the rest of the path. As far as we know, it's the first reversal of the Major Arcana's course in the history of the Tarot. And it made perfect sense for a Witches' Tarot.

We were on the ancestral path of initiation. A universal shamanic process, its direction is down and into oneself, into the womb of Mother Earth, not upward into the Father's heaven. Then, transformed, enlightened, and embodying the Divine, we return to a world we now recognize is also divine.

Initiation is a ritual well known to British Traditional Witches, many other traditions, and Indigenous peoples. It's also a natural part of life, often dismissed as a "mid-life crisis," though it can happen at any point. Whether deliberate or inadvertent, the process challenges and transforms us *if* we work with it. It's always a spiritual journey to our authentic self, and to a sacred world.

On this path of initiation, the Pilgrim/initiate is unmade in order to be made again. The artifices of ego and social conditioning are dismembered, the wounds of childhood and culture begin to heal, and the Pilgrim, guided and aided along the way by loving and compassionate Spirits, teachers, deities, and wise ones, gives birth to her empowered, enlightened, and embodied self.

The Pilgrim's path through the Major Arcana took her, and us, into the magic circle—away from the illusory man-made world and into the natural world, into Spirit, and *back* into the natural world and her natural self. We all come from Spirit and return to Spirit, but the journey of the soul is *through* life, through the Earth, through all the challenges, blessings, and magic of manifestation. So, the Pilgrim descends into the heart of our humanity and returns to the divine embodiment of Creation. It's the path of life, lived consciously and with reverence, in the body and from the heart. It's the path of the Divine taking form *through* Creation and *through* us. The Pilgrim discovers that there is no split between Spirit and World, for both exist within *her*. On this path, enlightenment is discovering that divine energy is *embodied* by each of us. Magic follows.

And so, on this universal journey, the Pilgrim changed genders, ages, and races, while remaining recognizable by the pentacle worn around their neck—an apple slice in which five seeds appear as their journey progresses. And as we journeyed, many of the Major Arcana took on new appearances, meanings, and teachings appropriate to a Witches' Wisdom Tarot. For example, the Lovers are no longer a heterosexual couple. Instead the card is Love, experienced and expressed by the Pilgrim and her familiar, one of the deck's guides, Fox. This was one of my favorite journeys to experience and texts to write, and its images were beautifully brought to life by Danielle. You can feel the love radiating outward from the Pilgrim and the Fox, encompassing the other *and* the world that holds them within the embrace of *its* love.

Another notable change is the banishing of the Devil. He belongs exclusively to the Abrahamic faiths, as their personification and projection of evil, and has no place in the world of Witches. Instead, the Ancestor, a revered figure in all Indigenous cultures, teaches about family, continuity, and maturity. The angel of Temperance is replaced by the Plant People, specifically the yarrow, who offer the gift of Healing. And the Hierophant is no longer arrayed in papal garb and the symbols of institutional authority. Instead, you'll meet the Wisdom Keeper, a teacher of utmost simplicity and clarity.

The world of our Witches' Major Arcana stretches further back in time than that of Rider-based decks, deeper into the Earth, and further out into a widening sense of the Sacred. Like the wisdom of the four elements, this new and yet most ancient world is populated with teachers and guides, deities and wise ones from the Arctic Circle to Africa, from the Fertile Crescent to the deserts of the American Southwest, all deeply compassionate, expansively wise, and firmly embodied.

We trusted that in sharing what they shared with us, we were respecting and honoring the universal wisdom of these guides and not appropriating their diverse cultural contexts. We saw and appreciated how the combination of diversity and unity created a gorgeous, healthy, and resilient tapestry reflecting the divine wisdom of Mother Earth.

Finally, at the "end" of the journey, the Pilgrim finds herself open-hearted, clear-headed, and fully present in her life. She is evolved, enlightened, and embodied. She is ready to go wherever life leads, for she knows that the world in which she lives is divinely alive and loving. It's this world to which she will return, ready to begin a new journey into a world re-enchanted by her presence and participation in its making.

This is the blessing path of the Major Arcana of the Witches' Wisdom Tarot. It is the path for all of us, for we are all the Pilgrim.

The Gift of Sight

There's a Witch, a wise one, within us all. And above all, a Witch must know and be true to themselves. Know yourself, and a divine world of wisdom, beauty, and blessings opens to you. A world of magic opens to you.

That magic is deeply healing. Witches have always been healers and the Witches' Wisdom Tarot is a healing deck. It will help you retrieve what's missing within and reconnect you to the life-nourishing and divine context in which you live. It offers countless paths into the wildness of Nature and your nature, and it will reconnect you to the wild magic of both. It will help you come home to your whole, holy, and natural self, and home to holy Mother Earth.

Many of her great teachings are within these cards, including a number of what I call "First Principles"—natural laws that are spiritual principles. One of the most fundamental, profound, and potentially transformative is that *all living things, when taking care of themselves, simultaneously make the world a better place for all life.*

The Witches' Wisdom Tarot reveals the countless ways in which Mother Earth, her elements and Spirit beings, her Plant and Animal children, are all collaborating in the support and care we need to heal, prosper, find our purpose, and manifest our fulfillment. This includes our valuable contribution to the wellbeing of the greater Life in which we live. And one of the ways that is accomplished is Nature's true Law of Abundance: *Take no more than you need, give back in kind, and there will always be enough for everyone.* This is Witches' wisdom.

In a human world so dangerously tipped out of balance by ego and greed, this wisdom is essential to the future of life on Earth. Fear, grief, and helplessness in the face of the destruction we're all seeing can be overwhelming, but the deeper truth is that everything we need for lives that are healthy, balanced, peaceful, abundant, and full of love is all around and within us. The Divine is embodied; all we need to do is ask for guidance. The Witches' Wisdom Tarot offers many blessings, but perhaps this is the most precious: *You are never alone. Ask and the Divine will answer.*

So, know that Spirits and guides, wise ones and deities are present to provide the guidance, love, support, and inspiration you need to create the life you were meant for and to help restore the life Mother Earth has taken 6 billion years to create. These guides have so much love and compassion for us all. They guided us in creating this deck. They will guide you in using it to create the life you were meant for.

Work with this deck and let it teach you. Let it help you to see within, to see realms of Spirit, to see the wonders of the natural world, and to see the beauty, wisdom, love, and divinity embodied by life, and by *you*. It will bless you with the gift of seeing the Sacred, and that is the source of all Witches' wisdom.

Magic will happen when you open your heart and allow that divinity to flow into you and from you into the world. The journey of the Witches' Wisdom Tarot will awaken the magic within you and awaken you to the magic of the world in which you live. Having just undertaken that journey, we promise you it will be an extraordinary adventure.

With love, blessings, and magic,

Phyllis Curott

Working with the Witches' Wisdom Tarot

The Witches' Wisdom Tarot is a magic mirror. Look into it and it will show you who you are and who you can be. Through its images and text, you'll find guidance for changing what's on the inside in empowering ways that will change what's on the outside.

Of course we all want to know the future—how much easier would that make our lives? The more you work with the deck, the more you'll come to know that fate is what you make it, or what you make of it. The deck will help you create the future you want and the Earth needs for life to continue in its sacred and wise ways.

Divination—Messages and Magic

To know who you are, you must know where you are—what's the context, the container, the web in which you live? What are the relationships your life depends on? What are the connections that nourish you, body *and* soul?

If you're taught that the Divine is other and elsewhere, you're wearing a blindfold and can't see what's right in front of you, around you, and within you—a living divinity that is the source and substance of Creation, of *you*. The core value at the heart of the Witches' Wisdom Tarot is the *union* of divinity and Creation, Spirit and Earth, energy and embodiment.

Divination shows us the forces hidden within us, in the past, present, and future. But Witches know there's more magic in the method. Most empowering of all, divination is a way to speak directly to the Divine and receive an answer that is always in our best interests.

Divination is proof that the Universe is alive, aware, and engaged with our wellbeing. It's deeply healing to realize that we're not alone, that there's always a wise, loving, and sacred presence to provide the guidance we need. All we have to do is ask.

Divination is a magical mirror for us to see ourselves through the eyes of the Divine. It enables us to see how our past, attitudes and emotions, patterns and projections are influencing our life in the present and setting the course for our future. It enables us to change, to choose, and to create our destiny.

Divination also helps us recognize our wounds *and* shows us how to heal them. And when we heal ourselves, we heal our future *and* the world. Divination shows us our gifts and how to cultivate them. And when we offer our gifts to the world, the world becomes a better place for us and for everyone. Divination empowers us to unlock the magic within us, to see circumstances and influences and the future so we can make the best choices and create our best possible life and the best possible world.

Knowing what may come is empowering. Not because we can control everything—in fact, we *can't* control everything. But we *can* control ourselves and how we respond to whatever takes place. *That* is how we begin to transform fate into destiny. And magic helps, because the first thing magic changes is us. Work with this deck and its magic will change you.

Make the Deck Yours

Danielle and I have offered a blessing spell for all the Witches' Wisdom Tarot decks, which you'll find inside the box, a spell for each deck to bring the guidance, insight, and blessings needed for the greatest good, happiness, and wellbeing. But you'll want consecrate your deck yourself. Here are a few simple steps to help you:

Consecrate Your Deck

- Work in a quiet and private space. If you wish and know how, cast a circle. Take the deck from its magical box and bag.
- Since it's never been used before, it's not necessary to purify the deck, but if you wish to, burn some (locally grown) sage and pass the deck through the smoke. Thank the sage when you're done.

- Hold the deck to your heart.
- Thank the deck for serving as your oracle, the voice of the Divine. Acknowledge its power to help you see clearly, to provide answers, and to provide loving guidance for living your best life and helping those who come to you for a reading. (Close your circle.)
- Sleep with the deck beneath your pillow or next to your bed for a full lunar cycle. This will help it to attune itself to you while you are uninhibited by conscious thought.
- Keep your deck someplace safe, wrapped in its magical bag, and, if you wish, its magical box. These will help it "hold its charge."
- You may also wish to purify your deck periodically, especially if you are reading for others. It's also a good idea to sleep with it periodically to recharge it and to express your gratitude to it.

Quick Pointers for Reading the Witches' Wisdom Tarot

Whether or not you're a Witch, mastering a new Tarot deck can seem daunting. But you'll find working with the Witches' Wisdom Tarot is a very organic process, as if you're remembering something you already know, rather than trying to master a foreign language of arcane symbols. Working with the cards, you'll find your intuition, understanding, and interpretations becoming increasingly accurate, personal, and meaningful.

You'll also see that the Major Arcana cards have new numbering to reflect their new order, but we've kept the old Rider Roman numerals, in parenthesis next to the new numbering, to help traditional Tarot readers and scholars.

Remain Upright

These cards are meant to be read upright. This is in keeping with the teaching of the element Air to focus on the positive. So, the cards don't have reverse meanings. They do reveal challenges, consequences, and even crises, particularly the "5" cards of all the elements. But these are framed with choices for positive outcomes.

Rather than reversals, each card has a *Counsel* explaining how to work with its *Wisdom*, including any difficulties or problems, for the best outcome.

Of course, if you prefer to include reversed cards in your readings, feel free to do so. We believe those meanings will be self-evident and you'll undoubtedly create your own as well.

Respond to the Imagery

The quickest way to master the deck is to work with one card at a time. (*See Single-Card Divination, p.32.*) You can start with a card that grabs your attention or evokes a strong emotion, randomly pick one, or proceed in the numerical order of the cards.

Begin by simply allowing yourself to respond to the imagery. Listen to what the animals, plants, deities, guides, wise ones, and especially the Pilgrim, whisper to you. Focus on parts of the image that call to you. What feelings and ideas do they conjure up in you? Allow space for whatever you feel, even if it's disturbing.

Ask yourself questions. Why is there a bird, a bear, a rose in the picture? Who is this figure? What are they doing? What are they feeling? What are they communicating to me? What does it make me feel? What does it mean? What does it mean to *me*?

It's useful to write your answers and impressions down in a journal.

Work with the Text

Once you have looked at the image, consider the text. It provides an explanation for the imagery and has other rich offerings too:

- The first is *Wisdom*, which provides a visionary explanation and experience of the card's meaning.
- The next is *Essence*, which provides quick, simple, key meanings useful for fast insights when doing readings for foresight or complex spreads.

- The third is *Counsel*, which is straightforward, practical advice on how to best apply the card's *Wisdom* and *Essence* to your question and your life.
- The final one is *Magic*—a concise and potent spell, potion, or other magical working to manifest the purpose of the card and your own intention.

It's important to read the texts and compare those meanings with the intuitive impressions you noted earlier. Intuition is the answer you find within yourself, but you'll need more than intuition to discern the full meanings of the cards—knowledge and experience are also essential. Experienced readers will note that there are some similarities between the Witches' Wisdom Tarot and the Rider deck, and you should feel free to bring your knowledge and personal interpretations to this deck. But the Witches' Wisdom Tarot is unique.

Take an Elemental Journey

One way to get to know the Minor Arcana is to start with the Ace of Air and progress through the entire element, including the four Shapeshifters—the Messenger, the Witch, the Craftsman, and the Goddess, powerful figures who bridge the realms of Spirit, Nature, and being human. Then move on to Fire, Water, and Earth to reconnect with the wisdom, power, and magic of the natural world around and within you.

Take a Soul Journey

Working with the Major Arcana offers another kind of profound spiritual journey. Just as the Minors help you connect with the divine wisdom of the natural world and your natural self, the Majors help you connect with your soul and its purpose.

Start with the World, 1 (Rider World XXI), where the Pilgrim's journey begins, then to Initiation, 2, and so on, to arrive at the Pilgrim, 0, now fully present, confident, and trusting in the Self that she, and you, have become. It's a deeply transformative journey. If you're prepared to make the commitment, work with one card a day over 22 days. Even as experienced practitioners, we found this tempo of journeying for the Major Arcana an extraordinary, life-changing experience and we felt as if we were in an altered state for the entire period. So, it's also *very* wise to take all the time you need to engage with the imagery, the text, and the impact of the cards on you.

Divination—Method and Mastery

The Witches' Wisdom Tarot will prophesize, foretell, and guide. How do you access its divinatory wisdom? Here are the steps for working with the deck:

Divination: Step by Step

- Work in a quiet, private space. Take a moment to ground your energy and clear your mind–a few slow, deep breaths will do it.

- Hold the deck to your heart and acknowledge its role as your oracle, your way of conversing with the Divine.
- Ask for clarity in receiving and understanding the reading.
- Ask your question. A simple, one-part question will work best. A good way to frame it is to ask: "What is my best possible outcome [describe the situation]?" You can also phrase your question (or follow-up question) this way: "What do I need to know/to do about [describe the situation] to achieve my best possible outcome?"
- Concentrate on your question and shuffle the cards until you feel ready to stop. The more you work with your deck, the more easily you'll recognize that feeling of readiness. If you are reading for someone else (the querant), you may wish to have them ask their question and shuffle the cards until they feel ready to stop. Don't riffle the cards, rather hold the deck in one hand while you randomly lift a few cards and then drop them back into the deck. Don't look at the pictures as you shuffle.

- Cut the deck into three separate piles on the table in front of you, then put the piles back together again in any order.
- Hold the deck to your heart and again focus on your question.
- You may wish to say: "My heart is open to your guidance. Thank you for your presence." Saying this focuses your faculties and charges you, the querant (if present), the space you're in, and the process of reading with sacred purpose.
- From the top of the deck, draw a single card or lay out a spread of cards (*for spreads, see p.31*).
- Look at the images. Take your time. Allow the pictures to speak to you. What feelings do they evoke? Does a particular part of a card's image hold your attention? What impressions or ideas come to mind? Allow yourself to associate freely.
- When you feel you've received as much as you can intuitively, use the text to help you further understand the meaning of the cards and your reading.

- In a multi-card spread, it takes time to see a coherent pattern in the various images and information and to discern meaning. It's helpful to ask yourself or your querant questions as you're seeking the significance of what's before you.

- Take time to reflect on the wisdom you've received. Allow thoughts, associations, and answers to arise. Insight might come in a flash of intuition or recognition, or it may take time to integrate what you've seen, read, and understood. Ultimately, the meaning is what is meaningful to *you*.

- Allow everything to move from your head into your heart. Don't rush this step.

- Don't ask the same question twice just because you want a different answer or don't like what you've been shown. You can, however, ask for clarification from another card or spread.

- Be sure to write down your impressions and interpretation and whatever guidance and insights you've received. Oracles can be cryptic and it may take time and patience to fully understand what the cards are showing you, or for it to come to pass, but the cards are always utterly honest.

- Thank the deck and put it safely away in its bag, and its box if you wish.
- You may want to put a card or cards on an altar, or someplace where you can see it/them, and reflect and meditate on the meaning. Or you could take a photo of it/them to consult during the day or keep in your journal.
- Remember, if you fail to follow the wise counsel you've received, the deck will stop giving it. It's equally important to remember that fate is what you make it or make of it.

Divination: Text First

You may prefer to work with the text of the cards first and then the images. Each section of the text–*Wisdom, Essence, Counsel, Magic*–offers distinct and useful guidance for divination.

- Formulate your question. What do you want or need to know?
- Run your finger along the edge of the book's pages until you feel pulled to open it. Or simply let it fall open.
- Read the page you've opened to and *then* study the imagery of the card and listen to your intuition to get your answer.

However you work, as you continue to do readings for yourself and others, your intuition will grow stronger and you'll begin to develop your own interpretations. In time, you'll discover new and deeper meanings, especially when you use the cards as visualization, meditation, and journeying portals (*see p.52*), and as you get to know their magic.

The Magic of the Witches' Wisdom Tarot

The Witches' Wisdom Tarot is filled with magic that must be experienced to be fully understood. The *Wisdom* section of each text is specifically written to evoke an altered state, opening your consciousness as you read. Each card is a portal into realms of Spirit and a path back into the magic of this realm. Working with the cards in this way will awaken you to the magic of the worlds in which you live and which live within you. So, in addition to the *Magic* in the cards' texts, here are five ways to work with the magic of the Witches' Wisdom Tarot:

Guided Visualization

Guided visualization helps you enter a card and its story, experience what's described and depicted, encounter the characters, creatures, teachers, and Spirits, learn the lessons, and receive the blessings they offer. Some of the texts begin before the image in the card, and some continue after. As you read, you'll find that there are natural spaces or opportunities for your own experiences, conversations, and conclusions. When the text ends, your experience may well continue on to reveal deeper and more personal insights.

Guided Visualization: The Practice

- You may wish to cast a circle, but, as always, work in a quiet, private space.
- Select your card. Take a few deep breaths. Study the imagery carefully.
- Read the accompanying *Wisdom* text aloud. You may want to record it and then listen to it with your eyes closed.
- As you do so, visualize yourself walking down a staircase and opening a large door.
- The portal into the world of the card will open and you'll enter. See the image of the card before you. The scene will change from a "still photo" to a moving picture, from a representation to a lived reality. You may need to pause in your reading or listening to allow events to unfold.

- If you wish, let your journey continue beyond the text's end.
- Thank all those you have encountered.
- Go back through the door and up the staircase.
- Journal about your insights.
- (Close your circle.)

Journeying

Journeying was essential to the creation of the Witches' Wisdom Tarot and so we recommend that you journey into the cards' imagery to experience their magic and meaning.

Journeying: The Practice

- You may wish to cast a circle, but as always, work in a quiet, private space.
- Select your card. Study the imagery, read the text, then study the imagery again.

- Turn off the lights, lie down, start a drumming audio, close your eyes, visualize, enter, and walk through a tunnel, and exit into the image of the card.
- Ask the Spirit of the card to appear to you and guide you. It will probably appear as one of the plant, animal, or Spirit beings depicted on the card.
- Ask to be shown what you need to understand about the card, or about your question.
- Allow yourself to experience whatever happens–remember, you're always with Spirits and guides who have great love and compassion for you, even if they offer challenges.
- When it's time to return, thank the wise one, Spirit, or guide who has assisted you and go back through the tunnel and into your body.
- Stretch, sit up, and journal about what you saw and learned.
- (Close your circle.)

Meditation

There is a long magical tradition of meditating on the imagery of Tarot cards to alter consciousness and encounter Spirit.

Meditation: The Practice

- As always, work in a quiet, private space.
- Breathe to quiet and clear your mind. Select your card. Study the imagery of the card. Take your time. It can be helpful to focus on an element of the image that attracts you.
- When you're ready, close your eyes. Use your meditation practice. If you don't have one, concentrate on taking deep, slow breaths in and out. When your attention drifts, bring it back to your breathing.
- Now visualize yourself walking down a staircase, through a door, and into the image.
- You've entered the Spirit realm of the card. Look around. What do you see? What do you hear? What's happening? The Pilgrim, wise ones, plants, and animals may engage with

you. You may become the Pilgrim or a wise one. Experience whatever follows.

- Thank all those you have encountered for whatever they have shared with you.
- Focus on your meditation technique, your breathing.
- Go back through the door and up the staircase.
- Open your eyes. Stretch. Write down your experiences.
- Read the card's text and reflect on it and your meditation.
- If you've been given advice, take it.

Invocation

An invocation is a powerful magical practice. It's a heartfelt calling upon a deity or Spirit, a wise one or guide for help, guidance, or whatever you need. In the Witches' Wisdom Tarot, the *Wisdom* text can be a powerful invocation of the being/energy depicted in the cards. You can read it in its entirety, or use what resonates for you in combination with your own language. Be patient and don't worry if you don't experience anything initially. Keep practicing, try different cards, and know that when the student is ready, the teacher appears.

Invocation: The Practice

- As always, work in a quiet, private space. You may wish to cast a circle, but it's not necessary.
- Select a card. Place it in front of you and focus on the figure in the image.
- Breathe deeply and feel your body relax and your mind grow still and focused. When you feel your heart open and a sense of longing for communion rising within you, you're ready to invoke.
- Read the *Wisdom* text or your adaptation of it.
- Look at the image.
- Read the text again.
- Close your eyes. Continue breathing deeply and fully. You may feel your heart filling with love,

power, or tenderness. You may feel goosebumps rising on your skin, electricity running through you, or a strong sense of presence arriving around or within you.

- Remain in that feeling of presence. Stay alert for the wisdom or blessing.
- When the feeling subsides, offer your thanks.
- Let any excess energies drain from the palms of your hands into the ground.
- (Close your circle.)
- Eat something and drink some water.
- Write down what you experienced.

Spellcasting

Magic happens when your heart opens and the Divine flows into you, through you, and into the world. Spells, rituals, and other practices give that divine energy shape and form in the world. There are many magical ways to work with the Witches' Wisdom Tarot, and each card has a suggested *Magic*. As you read the texts, particularly for the Major Arcana, you'll discover rhyming sentences that capture key teachings and magic in the cards and that you can add to the suggested *Magic* as chants. You can use the rhyming lines as written, add to them to personalize them, or write your own. Whichever you do, be patient. Remember, the first thing that magic changes is you. Act in accord with your intention and when your magic manifests, give something back.

Witches' Wisdom Tarot Spreads

A Tarot spread may give you a lot of information and, depending on its complexity, require you to reflect on the relationships between the cards to fully understand the answer to your question. This is a skill that comes with practice. You may already have it, but the meanings of this deck are often unique, so it may take time to fully understand what it's showing you. Since it's quite organic, the answer to your question may, however, also be clear to you immediately.

A spread may also address a very different issue than the one you asked about. If this happens, it's important to pay attention, because the deck wouldn't bring another matter to your attention if it weren't important.

Always remember, the cards don't predict the inevitable. Rather, they show you a probable outcome based upon your current and future circumstances and, most importantly, your attitude, expectations, and emotions. Readings help you see yourself and your circumstances. They make things clear to you. They provide the guidance you need to make choices and changes to create the future *you* want.

Single-Card Divination

Though not technically a *spread*, this is a wonderful practice that can make every day easier and more magical. It's also one of the best and most organic ways to learn the meanings of the cards. And it will nourish your Spirit to start and end your day with divine guidance and the optimism that connection gives you.

- Begin by acknowledging the deck as your oracle. Ask for its guidance, focus on your question, and shuffle the cards.
- One of the most productive questions to ask is: "What do I need to know to have the best day possible?"
- When you're ready, pull a card.
- Study the picture and allow your intuition to speak.
- Read the text and reflect on how it matches your intuitive impressions.
- Consider how the card answers your question. Sometimes the reply may seem cryptic or ambiguous, but the *Counsel* is very straightforward. Remember that the cards are wise advisors with a perspective outside the normal limits of space and time and so you may have been given a deeper, more complex, and more useful answer than a simple "Yes" or "No."
- Write down your question and a few key words of interpretation. Take a picture of the card to

look at during your day. Pay attention to how the guidance is helpful.

- At the end of the day, journal about your question, the card you received, its interpretation, your intuitions, the day's events, and how the message you received helped you.

Three-Card Spread

The three-card spread is a classic way to read the Tarot, especially when you are seeking a view of the future. It reveals a key past influence, the essential present circumstance, feeling, or attitude that is influencing the question, and, based on these, the probable future outcome.

- As always, begin by honoring the oracle.
- Focus on your question, shuffle the cards, cut the deck three ways, reconstitute it, and select the three cards on the top. Or shuffle the deck and pull three cards randomly.

- Lay them out face up in front of you, one at a time. The first card is placed on the left and is the past. The second card, in the center, is the present. The third card, on the right, is the future.

- If you wish, you may ask one more question for clarification, such as: "What do I need to do/ change to achieve the best possible outcome?" and draw three more cards.
- Use your intuition and the text to interpret the answer.
- Reflect and journal about the answer.

THE COMPASS ROSE READING AND SPELL

This is a very special spread I received for the Witches' Wisdom Tarot. Working with it, I found it provided many useful insights. It can also be used as a helpful spell.

The cards are laid out twice in a circle around two cards that symbolize the reader/querant and the question (*see p.66*).

The first circle (cards 1–6) describes current influences.

The second (cards 7–11) describes the best course of action and likely outcome.

You can lay out this spread on a table or, when you feel ready, as a way of casting a magic circle around you. The reading then becomes a spell for insight, transformation, optimism, and manifestation. Either way, proceed as follows:

- Decide on your question.
- Honor the oracle.

- After shuffling the cards, making three piles and reconstituting the deck, take cards off the top and place them in the following positions:

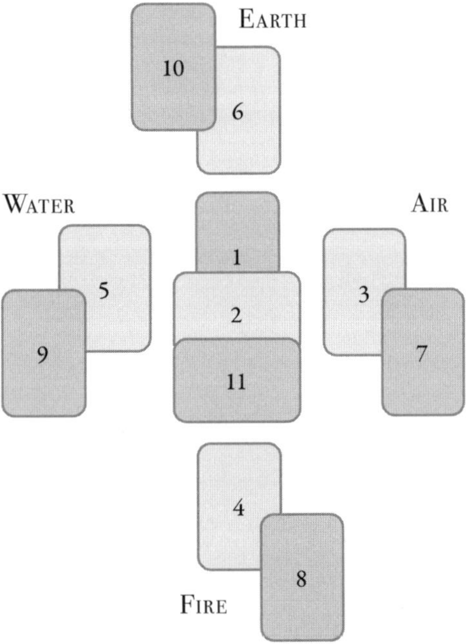

1. The first card is placed in the center. This is you or the person you're reading for. It is known as the querant card. As with all the cards you draw, study the image, note your impressions, then read the text of this card. The *Essence* may be a useful way of gaining quick and concise information, but you may wish to read the entire text for a complete understanding.

2. A second card is placed horizontally across the querant card. This is the question, obstacle, or goal of your reading or spell. It is always helpful to frame the question by asking what you need to know or understand about the current question or situation. If you are working a spell, pre-select the card that represents the goal of your spell.

3. The third card is placed to the right of the querant. This is the card of Air; of the querant's attitudes and thinking about the question and how their thinking is influencing the probable outcome; of unconscious patterns and conditioned thinking, especially about self-love; of communication issues around the question

or the querant; and of the querant's awareness of Love.

4. The fourth card is placed below the querant. This is the card of Fire and the energy with which the querant is approaching the question–fear or determination, aggression or joy, anger or courage. It provides insight into the questioner's confidence, willpower, and how they are working with their own energy and life force to influence the outcome.

5. To the left of the querant, the fifth card is the card of Water. It provides information about the feelings and emotions that the querant has about the question. It is also the position of ancestral and family emotional patterns, the messages passed on to us that influence how we feel about ourselves and others, the dreams we have for ourselves and the future. In addition, it describes issues relating to the question that involve relationships, the home, and matters of the heart, and how the body is expressing the querant's feelings.

6. The sixth card is placed above the querant. This is the place of the Earth and is about the practical influences at play–financial factors, work and body issues, including health. It gives an insight into how the querant is manifesting their purpose, making their way in the world, and expressing their creativity and self-worth, and what actions they are taking that relate to the question.

- After looking at the present circumstances in each of these areas of influence, lay out a second circle of four cards (cards 7–10) on top of the first one, from Air to Earth.

7. The second Air card provides the querant with guidance on how best to think about the question, what attitudes will be most helpful, and how love is best expressed.

8. The Fire card provides guidance regarding the right energies to use to transform the situation to best advantage.

9. The Water card counsels how to experience, embody, and express emotions, while

reminding that feelings aren't facts, but can be changed to create better outcomes.

10. The Earth card shows the querant how to ground mind, energy, and emotions in concrete actions that will heal wounds and limitations and help generate positive results.

- Remember, the cards you draw for each direction may be a different element than that of the direction's element. For example, you may pull a Fire card for the second Air position. This will direct you to look at how your thoughts affect your energy, and vice versa. Or you may draw a Major Arcana card for Earth, which will require you to consider how to heal, embody, and act upon the guidance of that card.

11. A final card should be placed in the center, horizontally, to show you what changes to expect and what the likely outcome will be if the cards' counsels are taken to heart. Take time to bring the image and its meaning into yourself. You may also wish to work the *Magic* in the final card's text.

- Whether as a reading or a spell, set your intention to take the counsel you've been given and see it clearly manifesting. When you're ready, with feeling and commitment say: "So mote it be!"
- Gather up the cards, which will open the circle (also called "closing"), i.e. end it. Thank the deck and the Divine for their guidance. And remember to act in accord with that guidance.

May your readings be clear, helpful, and inspiring, may your magic awaken, and may the future exceed your expectations! *So mote it be!*

INTERPRETATIONS OF THE CARDS

THE MINOR ARCANA

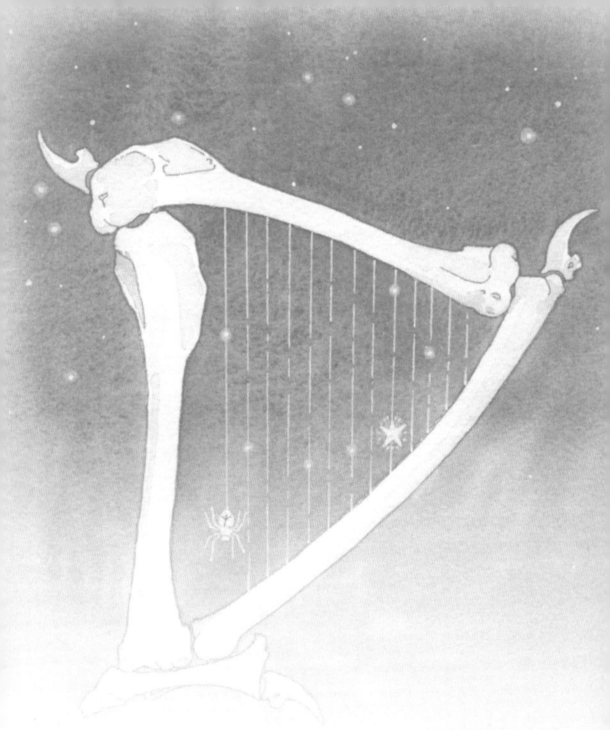

AIR

Ace of Air
~ Wind Harp ~

Wisdom

Air, the first vibration from which everything proceeds into manifestation, the element awakening us to the consciousness of Creation, to infinite connection. Between the bones of what was first created, the winds of summoning stir the strings woven by spiders and filled with stars. A deafening noise roars through, a cosmic chord of sounds piled one upon the other. Together, they are almost music. The swish of a breeze and rustle of leaves, the melody of birdsong and howl of a storm, and all the sounds in between.... This is the magic of the Wind Harp. It's Love.

Essence

Listen, awareness, divine Love. Say what's in your heart.

Counsel

Air is the element of consciousness, intelligence and intuition, reflection and communication, laughter and music, infinite connection and love. But silence comes first. If you're talking, you cannot listen. The mind is always confronted with choices, and so it chatters. But don't rush to action. Slow down. The answer you're seeking is waiting for you to hear it.

Magic

Go outside on a windy day. Feel the Air on your skin, messing up your hair, singing in your ear. What do you hear? Listen to the love songs the wind sings to you. What is the enchantment of the moment? What is the song in your heart? The spell you long to chant? Give it voice and let the wind carry it into Creation.

2 of Air

~ Vulnerability ~

Wisdom

Pay attention. Things are more than they seem. A brown and prickly chestnut trembles, rolls, and uncurls into a Hedgehog. The Hedgehog breathes, its tiny lungs reflected in the great Tree towering above it. The breath of life moves back and forth between them. Two Crows, sitting high up in the branches, look down with curiosity. They, too, are breathing with the Tree. Everything is connected by the breath of life. Leaves stir gently in the wind that carries, connects, and whispers Witches' wisdom: "The Divine is a breath away."

Essence

Openness, connection. Trust yourself. Trust life.

Counsel

It's time to let go, to trust, to allow yourself to be vulnerable. Breathe and the trees breathe with you, exchanging the breath of life with you. Breathe and be aware that you are always nurtured by the world to which you are connected. It's time to open to the safety of ever-present divine Love. All you need to do is breathe it in.

Magic

Work with the Air to clear your mind. Breathe slowly, fully, deeply. Your breath is the breath of the trees, and the trees are the lungs of the world.

Inhale. Every breath connects you to the trees and the world. Exhale. Allow the love within you to open outward. Listen to the wisdom the wind brings you.

3 of Air

~ Rise Up ~

Wisdom

Three Herons Rise Up from dark and troubled Waters, up through the clouds swirling about them. They are undisturbed by the wild winds on which they soar, their wings more powerful than any turbulence. Their Spirits are those of ancient dragons, though their bodies are covered not by scales, but by soft down and fine feathers. Buffeting doesn't impede them or plunge them downward. They have the gift of flight, the ability to rise above strife to the unseen and shining Sun.

Essence

Rise above. See from a new perspective. Free yourself.

Counsel

You have the power to rise above whatever difficulties you are confronted with. Begin by shifting your thinking. View the situation from a distance. See beyond the moment to the bigger picture. Problems shrink when seen from this perspective. Ask yourself if in one year, five years, ten years, you'll remember what troubles you today. Seeing the future offers you a solution *today*. Put on the wings of foresight and let them carry you upward.

Magic

Find a feather. Accept it as a sign of the future you are going to create. Hold it to your forehead. Focus on your intention. Speak from your heart. Honor the feather as a power object to help you envision and create your future.

4 of Air

~ Sanctuary ~

Wisdom

On a narrow cliffside ledge or in the branches of the tallest Tree, high above the world and just beneath the floor of heaven, the Eagle makes its nest. It's a place of refuge, a place where wings can fold, eggs keep warm, and fledglings hatch. It's a place from which to view the world far and near, a home from which to soar when refreshed and ready. Even the Eagle, the most powerful and honored bird of prey, of power and freedom, needs a place to rest.

Essence

Refuge. Withdrawal from struggle and conflict. Rest, self-care, renewal.

Counsel

It's time to come home to yourself without any disguises, to look within and see yourself with self-love. Give yourself time and space to revisit your memories and reflect on your choices, to know and accept yourself, to nourish and protect what needs care. Welcome yourself home. From this place of safety and rest, you can decide where to go, what to do, what to create next.

Magic: Cleanse and Bless Your Home

Create an incense: take equal parts dried local sage, hyssop, pine resin, horehound, and nettle root, grind to a coarse powder, and burn. Fan the incense with a feather as you move around the perimeter of your home, encircling your nest and blessing it with love, peace, and happiness. Come to rest in the center.

5 of Air

~ Sacrifice ~

Wisdom

Two long-eared Owls have exchanged freedom for family. Driven by love and instinct, the mother Owl spreads her wings to shelter the young as the father stands guard. Life is full of trade-offs, of exchanging one thing of value for another. Owls sacrificed the protection of fat and feathers, but received the blessing of silence; hushed wings leave them vulnerable to Water and weather, unable to hunt in the rain, but quiet flight makes them the greatest hunters in the night. And the Owl is wise. It's the guide on the journey to self-awareness and to awareness beyond the self.

Essence

Sacrifice, acceptance, integrity, higher purpose.

Counsel

This is a card of choice and consequence. In life, we often have to give up one thing for another. Consider what you've been asked to Sacrifice. Certain roles, like being a parent, an apprentice, or the one in charge, may require you to give more than you seem to receive. Love comes with responsibilities. What you take on, what you give yourself to, what you serve will create your character and your life. Be sure it's worthy of you.

Magic: Practical Magic

Take stock of what you do in your daily life for your own convenience or comfort that causes harm elsewhere. What would you be willing to Sacrifice to cause less harm or even make things better for others, for Mother Earth?

6 of Air
~ Balance ~

Wisdom
Where Air and Water meet, two Swans preside, creatures of the wing equally at home where they must swim. Messengers of the Goddess, they carry missives and prayers between the worlds. Safe between the devoted pair, their four Cygnets swim. Love created them, protects and nourishes them, teaches them to swim and fly. But a Fox waits upon the shore. If they take to the land before maturity, they could become prey. This does not make the Fox evil. Fox and Swan are equal parts of Mother Earth's Law of Balance. All of Creation is held in the right measure for Life to flourish.

Essence
Divine communication. Development, useful limits. Danger for the unprepared.

Counsel
Open your heart to the Goddess and attend to the messages She's sending you. Take pride

in your spirituality, trust your intuition, honor your dreams. But don't rush into things you're not ready for and don't despair if your efforts don't succeed. Allow yourself time to grow. Cultivate your skills, your wisdom, your heart. Nurture your dreams. When you're ready, the Universe will offer you the opportunities for which you've prepared.

Magic

Practice folding an origami Swan. Write a prayer to the Goddess. Find a body of Water where there are Water birds. Read your prayer aloud. Fold the paper into the Swan. Hold it to your heart. When you're ready, float it on the Water. It will carry your prayer to the Goddess. Offer bread or birdseed.

7 of Air

~ Witch's Ladder ~

Wisdom

A Witch's Ladder is a spell to make a dream come true. Seven feathers, each from a different bird, are knotted to a cord, then tied to a tree branch.

Each feather is a charm, free to flutter, spin, and dance in the wind, yet all are connected to the Earth by an enchanted hagstone tied at the end of the cord. Each feather has come to a Witch as a sign, a signal, an answer. A Witch's Ladder gives them all back, with gratitude for the guidance given by a wise and loving Universe.

Essence

Clues, signs, insight, gratitude, offerings. Magic is afoot.

Counsel

Messages are arriving from the Sacred. Signs and synchronicities are offering guidance to help you manifest your future. Pay attention. If guidance isn't followed, it's no longer given. But offering thanks sets magic in motion. A Witch's Ladder asks and offers simultaneously. Honor the divine laws of Nature and magic happens.

Magic: Create a Witch's Ladder

Reflect on your goal. Take seven feathers that have come to you as signs and recite your intention as you tie them to a cord. Knot a hagstone or other weight to the bottom. Declare:

"So mote it be!" Tie your Ladder to the branches of a willing tree or hang it in your home. When your magic manifests, return the feathers to Mother Earth with thanks.

8 of Air

~ Clarity ~

Wisdom

An Eagle flies high above the Earth, just beneath the Sun. It sees the vast expanse of land and the tiniest detail within it. Its vision is all-encompassing, precise, and clear. From the ground, it seems distant and insignificant, and yet in an instant it can swoop down upon its prey. Hidden from view, a tiny Wood Mouse goes about its day. Guided by an instinct equally powerful and sure, it lives beneath the sheltering elfdock, which blossoms like the Sun above the little creature's head. From their different vantage points, both beings see the world with perfect Clarity.

Essence

Honesty, objectivity, introspection, self-awareness.

Counsel

You need to be utterly honest with yourself. If you're kidding yourself about what you actually want, you may get very unexpected results. Notice how ideas and fears can limit you. Conditioning or circumstances can contribute to negative thinking, but your mind has the power to free you. Regardless of the circumstances, see what's true *and* possible, so you can make the best choices.

Magic: Banishing

Write down a problem that you're struggling with. Then, when the Sun is high in the midday sky, burn the problem paper. Look at the smoke rising and disappearing and see your troubles disappearing too. Now look carefully at the world around you. Look for a sign that will show you what you need to know or do next.

9 of Air

~ *Transition* ~

Wisdom

The desert is so hot and dry, everything vibrates, including the Air. The flowers are finished and the fruit has ripened, fallen, and broken open on the ground. Everything is just past its prime and beauty is turning to decay. The sickly sweet smell of spoiled perfection is unsettling, and so is the vibrating Air. Thousands of bees swarm and buzz. It's time to move. There's not enough food in the area, or the hive is overcrowded, or filled with parasites and disease, or a new queen has been born. Things have ended. Something new is beginning. It's natural. The mystery is making magic with the power of time.

Essence

Endings, time for change. Move on. Begin anew.

Counsel

Death comes to all living things, to all our human vanities. It's frightening. What's the antidote to nightmares? Open your eyes. There's a divine being within you that has outgrown the past and is ready for a new life. Learn what you need to and move on.

Magic

Take an empty jar and fill it a quarter full with dried peas or beans. Tighten the lid. Bless it with feathers, incense, and wind. Rattle and spin, make a great noise, release the past, chant the future, stir the Air with the energy of your soul vibrating to its purpose. When you feel your energy peak, release your magic with a final "*Huzzzzzzzzzzah!*" and drop to the ground like ripened fruit.

10 of Air

~ Murmuration ~

Wisdom

There's a wondrous spectacle in the invisible Air where everything is connected: a Murmuration of Starlings has appeared to fill the Autumn sky with blissful whirling. It's dusk, the Sun is sitting on the edge of the Earth, and the shapeshifting flocks are filling the world with their magic, every bird connected to every other bird by a mystery. They are rippling, spinning, plunging, and ascending in unison, the pattern transformed in an instant as 100,000 Starlings turn together as one. In the presence of magic, we bear witness to the wind between the stars, the divine Love that connects all things and fills the world with wonder beyond understanding.

Essence

Wonderment, intuitive harmony, communion, consciousness of divine Love.

Counsel

It's time to let go of the need for explanations, reasons, and rational understanding. There's wisdom in your heart that's longing to be free. You're on a journey to awareness beyond the self, inspired by something mysterious and beautiful that is part of you and greater than you. Stand in awe of the divinity beyond explanation. Let your Spirit soar.

Magic

Find a Murmuration near you—starlings flocking, a school of flashing fish, trees moving in the wind, heavy snowfall, a rock concert. Move with it and give yourself to the ecstatic energy of divine collective joy.

Messenger of Air

Wisdom

Formed of whispers, quicksilver, and moonlight, the Messenger of Air is shapeshifting as swiftly as he comes and goes—a swan, a hawk, a crow, a clever disguise to trick the eyes as he carries messages between the worlds. Faster than the wind, he can be summoned by words of magic, but only from a heart as pure as his. It's a blessing to catch a glimpse of this Messenger of wonder, and if your words catch his ear, he will transport the dreams you long to manifest and return with the answers to your prayers.

Essence

Dream, ask, believe. Anything is possible.

Counsel

Remember your childhood dreams? How you could fly? How you woke in the morning, knowing anything was possible? Anything *is* possible. Believe in your dreams and the magic within you will reawaken. Ask for help with the open-heartedness of a child and the Universe will give wings to your dreams.

Magic

When the new Moon appears, write a short rhyming spell that names a dream you long for. Feel what it will be like to have it come true. Go out into the moonlight and chant your spell until you feel the Air Messenger is there to carry it into realms of Spirit. Give thanks, go to bed, and pay attention to dreams at night and signs during the day.

Witch of Air

Wisdom

Whirling a bullroarer to makes the winds howl and blow, the Witch of Air spins her ecstatic enchantments into being. Amid the seeming tumult of sound and motion, her mind is clear. Her feathered cloak opens as she whirls, chanting visions into form—a lunar moth, a blossoming rose, a sigh of surrender, a starry night. Wings extended to encompass the world, the Witch of Air sings her spells to summon dreams into being. She is making magic. Her mind and heart are in harmony, and the song she sings is Love.

Essence

Envisioning, enchantment, ecstasy, devotion, divine Love.

Counsel

What are your intentions for your life? Everything—ventures and adventures, inventions and works of art—begins with an idea. What your mind can conceive, you can bring into being. But you need to love what you envision. Love is the energy you need to give form to your intention, expression to your purpose, and to bring your dreams to life. What do you love?

Magic

Create an incense with equal parts frankincense and myrrh. Burn it, and when the smoke billows all around you, dance and chant:

She changes everything She touches
and everything She touches changes.

Spiral outward and clockwise, then reverse, spiraling counterclockwise into the center of the spiral. Raise your arms and ask the Spirit of the Witch of Air to aid you in manifesting your magic. *So mote it be!*

Craftsman of Air

Wisdom

Intelligent and intuitive, instinctive and contemplative, the mind works best when it's open. The world will open for a Craftsman who knows that Nature doesn't require mastering once the mind has been mastered. The Craftsman of Air is studying the mysteries hidden in the shapes that Spirit takes, the spiral shells and spinning galaxies, unfurling ferns and coiling DNA. He is studying the languages of math, patterns, and poetry. Numbers and images materialize in his mind, on the page, and in the Air, evaporating swiftly, but leaving traces of beauty. The cosmic blueprint is visible everywhere—the Golden Mean hidden in Nature's conjuring. The Craftsman is learning magic.

Essence

Study, hidden truths, divine expressions, and embodiments.

Counsel

Magic is more than special effects. It's more than formulas and incantations, though those are useful in achieving self-mastery. Magic will not grant you the power to control the world, but it may grant you the ability to understand it, and yourself. And with understanding will come reverence, respect, and responsibility. A Witch is a Craftsman who knows that the first thing magic changes is oneself.

Magic

Gather a snail's shell, a nautilus shell, a sunflower, pine cone, pineapple, and cauliflower. Study their spiral patterns. Look at a spider's web. Look into the night sky. Look at photos of hurricanes. Look in a mirror. Look at your fingers, your body, the body of a dolphin, a starfish, a honeybee. Look and learn the magic of Life.

Goddess of Air

Wisdom

Ancient and ever-present, the Goddess of Air spins the fabric of infinite connection. She untangles the past, repairs the present, and weaves the future. She is Grandmother Spider, braiding destiny with the passage of time. Fingers and feet on the web of Life, She feels every movement, senses the smallest vibration, knows what lies beneath the surface. In one hand, She holds a spindle; in another, a knife; in another, a sistrum, to set the tempo for the billion heartbeats allotted to all living beings before She cuts the threads and weaves the magic of Life again.

Essence

Interconnectedness. Fix your relationships. Cut ties, release the past.

Counsel

Your life is interwoven with those of your family, friends, and community. The Goddess of Air asks: "Do you recognize how many connections tie you to others and to the natural world on which you depend? What energies flow between you and others? What are you sending out? Taking in? Giving back? How can you cut the ties that don't serve your life? How can you mend those that do? How can you nourish your relationships with the community of Creation?"

Magic

Braid three colored ribbons together: one for the past, one the present, and one for the future. Chant as you braid:

> *[Something positive] from the*
> *past, [something positive] in the*
> *present, [something positive] for*
> *the future, together I weave.*

Hang your braid up to remind you of your power to create your life.

FIRE

Ace of Fire

~ *Cauldron of Community* ~

Wisdom

The Sun rises and its warmth draws forth life from the Earth. Fire is the spark of Life. Fire is the power of transformation. Fire is Spirit. Approach Fire with reverence and it will show you its true nature, purpose, and power. Since the beginning of time, we have built our communities around Fire. In the center of our circle, placed with care upon the Fire we tend, the Cauldron of Community makes the magic that sustains Life. Fire is there for all of us. Fire is joy.

Essence

Vitality, sharing, community, joy, rejoicing.

Counsel

Fire blesses us with the light to see the goodness and grace in ourselves, in others, and in our community—human and local, natural and global. It allows others to see the goodness in us. Fire is the source of joy, the energy to create.

There is a divine spark within you, inspiring you to create your life, inspiring you to serve your community. Fire is the energy that brings a community together, creating harmony, balance, and peace, creating the future. A community working together to redress our relationship with power has the potential to change the world.

Magic

Take a large pot and cook something for those you love and those you don't know. Gather people together. Feed them, feed yourself, feed the future. Ask Fire for its help, stir the Cauldron, and make the magic of belonging and sharing.

2 of Fire

~ Beyond Fear ~

Wisdom

The Sun's heat beats fiercely upon desert sands, where danger, Scorpions, and Snakes reside. One wrong step and destinies collide. Plants are prickly and Serpents are venomous; the Sun has distilled their balms and venom and all the sensations they provoke into concentrated power. Tread carefully, but walk on, for the thorniest plants contain the most potent medicine, and rattling Snakes carry prayers for rain. To live, one must honor Life with all its challenges, and to cure others, one must first be wounded. Fear is transitory; Witches' wisdom takes its place.

Essence

Challenges, danger, doubts. Facing and overcoming fear.

Counsel

Don't let fear paralyze or weaken you. Instead, use it to sharpen your focus and your thinking. Stop telling yourself that you can't. The courage to create your life is never about the absence of fear. The secret is to feel the fear and act anyway. Whatever scares you—failure or success, not being good enough, heartbreak, or the unknown—feel it, thank it for protecting you, and move through it. There's much to be gained from a small amount of pain. Courage and freedom, empathy, and destiny await you.

Magic

Do something that you've told yourself you can't. Repeat three times:

If I can't, then I must. Fears into
freedom, doubts into trust. Scary
Snake into mighty Dragon.

3 of Fire

~ Lights in the Darkness ~

Wisdom

Mired in gloom, the swamp is dark and dangerous. Three Will-o'-the-Wisps appear, glistening in the mist and the Water. Do they light the way through the shadowy unknown or lure the unwary traveler into a treacherous bog? Do you trust the pixie Lights to guide you? In old tales, being "pixie-led" is often considered a bad thing—but not by those who have followed and returned changed.

Essence

Uncertainty, intuition, faith, guidance.

Counsel

In the face of the unknown you may feel anxious and afraid. But is a safe passage what you actually need? This is your moment to let the pixie Lights lead you from the well-worn path into the wilderness. It's in the dark wood where the straight way is lost that we find ourselves. It's scary and exciting, but fear is only excitement that hasn't received permission. Let yourself be guided.

Magic

Be patient. Pixies may have a long way to travel from their native Dartmoor, and they need to trust you before they will appear. Welcome them. Pour fresh cream into a bowl, spread honey on fresh bread, place these offerings in your garden, or at your door or window, then dance and chant:

> *Come to me, come to me, flying on a honeybee, in this place you're safe from harm, guide me with your pixie charm.*

And don't confuse the smallness of their size with the measure of their magic.

4 of Fire

~ *Hearth Fire* ~

Wisdom

Like the Sun, the Vixen has created life, warming and nourishing her cubs with her love and Nature's gifts. Like her cubs, you have a place of peace, safety, and comfort. The scent of woodsmoke rises from that place that calls you home. There, the sacred Hearth Fire warms the space, the food, and the hearts of all who gather round it. Gaze into its flames and Fire will reveal its true nature and yours: the joy of life. Welcome home.

Essence

Home, welcome, safety, comfort, family.

Counsel

When you come home to yourself, a light shines within you. Tend that light, that warmth, that divine Fire, and you'll feel the comfort, brightness, and lightness of your Spirit. Others will also. Welcome your family, friends, and community to your Hearth Fire and your heart.

Magic: A Protection Spell for Hearth and Home

Grind a handful of dried St John's wort into a powder. Mix with a teaspoon of salt. Light a Fire in the hearth, or set an incense charcoal on a heatproof burner in the heart of your home. Put a pinch of the mix on it to burn. Chant or sing:

Blessed be this Fire, blessed be
this home. Keep us safe within
and also as we roam.

Circle your house, outside if possible, inside if not, sprinkling the mix as you continue chanting the blessing, creating a circle of protection around your home.

5 of Fire

~ Choice ~

Wisdom

The forest is ablaze. Are the trees adorned in Autumn's colorful glory, a verdant and varied community living in harmony, bathed in the honeyed sunlight that makes all things thrive? Or is the forest burning, with our aggression, destruction, and misunderstanding spreading like wildfire? Fire creates and Fire destroys. This is a moment of Choice and change. The course of Life hangs in the balance. Look more closely. Which do you see? Which do you choose?

Essence

Warning, abuse of power. Choice. Organic change.

Counsel

This is a card of warning. It shows both sides of Fire: one that is natural and life-sustaining; the other reflecting humanity's abuse of the element. Which do you see? To change the world, you must first change yourself. How do you hold your own power? Do your wounds make you selfish, angry, even abusive, or draw those who are? Take time for reflection and healing. Find ways to honor and harness your Fire that will contribute to your own happiness and to creating an empowering, supportive, and diverse community, wherever you find it. Small changes lead to big ones.

Magic

This is practical magic toward healing humanity's relationship with power. Simply perform an act of community service in a way that feels appropriate, whether it's picking up litter or spending half an hour talking to someone who's lonely. Make a commitment to this positive, empowering, and joy-creating action and follow through.

6 of Fire

~ Light on Water ~

Wisdom

Dragonflies pivot and hover, darting faster than the eye can perceive. Everything is in motion—the Sun above, reflected in the rippling currents below; the Light dancing on the Water. Harmony is made visible. Sunlight shines through prisms of Air and Water, and hidden colors appear. A ray of Light opens into the rainbows of Nature's magical perfection. Is the sunbeam one or many? Particle or wave? The answer is "*Yes.*" Stay and watch the dancing Light transcending all duality, immortalized in its essential peace, purity, and clarity.

Essence

Lightness of being. Illumination, clarity. Be present in the moment.

Counsel

There's a luminous quality of being that shines from everything, including you. It can be hard to find when the pressures of daily life weigh upon you. But Nature is constantly offering you a mirror in which to see the Light that shines in you. Every part of Creation is a revelation of divinity. Just look.

Magic

Hang a prism in your window, then wait and watch. You may not see a beam of Light enter the faceted crystal, but you may see a rainbow exit. Watch it bounce upon your walls, ceiling, floors. Hold your hands up and let it play upon your skin. Be present. Play with the Light and the rainbows, and when the day is overcast, remember the dancing, radiant beauty.

7 of Fire

~ Benevolence ~

Wisdom

The Sun is shining and the world is warm and beautiful and full of wisdom. Among blooming red roses, a Lion waits to offer medicine that will transform your life. Walk together and learn that strength is not just shown by feats of courage or acts of violence. It takes strength to be a compassionate guardian who nurtures and protects with quiet, determined integrity. Benevolence fills the garden of the world and life blossoms.

Essence

Conviction, integrity, resolve. Serenity. All will be well.

Counsel

You're living in a time of challenges, when many precious truths have been forgotten. But look within and look to the natural world, and you'll find the convictions and values that will give your life meaning. Embodying and defending these doesn't require anger, violence, or aggression, but clarity, commitment, and consistency. *That* is integrity, and it will give you strength *and* joy.

Magic

Cut a slice of wood about 2 inches (5 centimeters) across. Drill a hole close to the edge and thread a red cord through it. Draw a rose, a lion, or a symbol you prefer on it with a permanent marker. Charge it with purpose: hold it to your heart, light a candle, and say:

I ask you to carry the energy of
courage and determination with me.

Feel the power of Fire in your heart, hand, and belly. When the candle burns out, thank the amulet for accepting the charge. Keep it with you.

8 of Fire
~ *Wake Up!* ~

Wisdom

Baboons have gathered to greet the Sun. They sit silently, waiting. The sky turns crimson as the blazing light rises from a slumbering Earth. The world is bathed in gold as the tribe rises, waving their arms and exclaiming ecstatically, as if they hadn't attended yesterday's dawn, or the one before, or every dawn since the beginning of time. And who is wiser? You, sleeping and unaware in your dark room, or your cousins, whom the Egyptians honored as gods? Wake Up and welcome the Sun.

Essence

Wake Up! You're alive and anything is possible. Celebrate.

Counsel

Wake Up! Each sunrise offers the chance to be grateful that you've been given another day of life. Today you have another chance to make the dreams you're working on come true, or to heal and begin anew. Every moment you're here, in this world, in your body, in the natural world, the Divine is embodied and offering you reasons to rejoice. Accept the invitation to Wake Up to the magic of your life.

Magic

Set your alarm and rise before dawn. Go outside. When the Sun appears, stand up. Take the Sun between your hands and bring it to your heart. Feel the Fire in the center of your being, awakening every cell and igniting the spark of your life. Honor the Spirit of Fire. Honor your own Spirit. Give thanks for another day and use it well.

9 of Fire

~ Alchemy ~

Wisdom

Life is the child of Sun and Earth. Energy and embodiment, each fulfills the other, and their unity dazzles, delights, and nourishes body and soul. The pattern of divine perfection unfolds: every seed becomes a stem, every stem bears a bud, every bud blossoms into a flower, every flower becomes a fruit. Cut the fruit open and behold the magic and the mystery: from one seed, now five are arranged in perfect symmetry as the star, the sign of ever-changing and eternal Life, abundant and generous. Share, eat, give thanks, and give back.

Essence

Revelation. Abundance. Reciprocity, generosity, gratitude.

Counsel

Look at all that you enjoy. Anything you want, you can have ... or can you? We're coming to the end of what unbridled Fire can do. Only so much can be consumed before there is nothing left. How much do you really need? Do all your possessions really satisfy your soul? It's time to live in accord with Nature's Law of Abundance: *Take no more than you need, give back in kind, and there will always be enough for everyone.*

Magic: An Abundance Talisman

Place five apple seeds on a square of green cloth. Tie it up with a gold ribbon and carry it with you. Next time you buy something for yourself, give something away to someone who needs and will value it. Energy must move correctly for magic to manifest.

10 of Fire

~ Spirit of Life ~

Wisdom

Even on the longest night, Fire burns sure and bright. Amid the bare branches of a dark wood, candles have been lit so that people may find their way home. Each small flame has been kindled as a prayer—profound, beautiful, and sacred. Together, the tiny lights combine to form a circle of safety and sanctuary, a world full of holy magic. Peace suffuses everything. Fire is Spirit itself. Joy is its blessing.

Essence

Sanctity, safety, light. Peace, joy, reverence.

Counsel

The power of Fire is found in countless small moments of joy, insight, gratitude, and kindness—the infinite number of tiny flames that together create the power of your Spirit. Observe and honor the forces that flow through your life, rather than fighting for power over them, and you'll arrive at the sacred place of sanctuary and reverence where peace and joy are found. Then the Spirit of Life will burn brightly in you and through you into the world, lighting the way for those who follow.

Magic

At the Winter Solstice, the longest, coldest, darkest night of the year, the spark of new life rests within the womb of the Great Mother. On this night, carve your name into a gold candle, along with a single word or symbol of your goal for the next cycle of becoming. Light it and honor your power to kindle Fire and bring blessings into the world.

Messenger of Fire

Wisdom

The Messenger—young, strong, and shining like the Sun whose sign is on his glowing shield—stands beside a huge Ram with golden horns—one strength, the other truth. Together, they look out across a world that is bright and new, filled with light and shimmering with heat and meaning. At the Messenger's feet, beneath the Earth's most ancient tree, a pine cone encompasses a blueprint of the future. His task has appeared. He picks it up and places it in his pocket. Energy courses through him. He is ready to spring into action. Truth requires light to be seen, and time to become wisdom.

Essence

Readiness. Signs have been given. Seize the moment.

Counsel

The Universe will speak to you with anything that is available, but you must pay attention or you'll miss the message. Learn the language of the Sacred, the vocabulary of symbols. Here is an ancient sign: the Scarab is the lowliest creature and serves the highest purpose. From deep within the Underworld, it rolls a ball of dung into the sky to become the Sun.

Magic

The Messenger appears with a question: "What lowly task have you undertaken that can show you your strength and determination and transform your life with power?" Your answer is the message that unleashes magic.

Witch of Fire

Wisdom

Deep within Mother Earth, a sacred cave is filled with heat and dreams. Swirling smoke conceals then reveals the Witch of Fire. The spark of Life burns in her eyes as she tosses bay leaves into a bowl of glowing embers. Fire dances as she summons visions. The mythic Snake wraps round the immortal Oracle as the Pythia looks into your heart. She knows what the future holds and what magic will create it. She knows how the spark of Life becomes flames of joy. But before she shares her precious wisdom with you, you must know yourself.

Essence

Look within. Know yourself. Find gold in the dark.

Counsel

The Fire Witch challenges you to discover what you truly want. It may not be what you first think. Look within and don't be blocked by what frightens you. There is gold in the darkness—lessons that will liberate your Spirit and empower you. When you recognize that, the Fire Witch will show you how to bring your dreams into being and fill your life with joy.

Magic: A Dream Pillow

Create a dream pillow. Hold dried mugwort, preferably organic, and ask it to work with you. Fill a small cotton bag with it or tie it in a cotton handkerchief. Ask your question. Ask for a sign, for a guide. Ask your dreams to help you. Place the dream pillow under your pillow. Go to sleep. When you wake up, before getting out of bed, write down everything you remember from your dreams.

Craftsman of Fire

Wisdom

Through darkness come the sounds of metal ringing and flames crackling, the hiss of steam rising, and the inescapable heat of Fire's magic. Amid flying sparks, the Craftsman of Fire appears, forging enchantments in the flames. He can make swords or plowshares, but prefers to make horseshoes. The forge is his altar, the smithy his temple, his work divinely wrought. Reverently transforming the elements of Mother Earth with the power of Fire, he has created the Cauldron of Community. Honor his creation, honor the Fire, honor the Craftsman, and he will make you his apprentice.

Essence

Work hard, hone your skills, pursue your calling. Trust your ability and your strength.

Counsel

There is power within you that has a purpose. Conditions may be challenging and you may have to work in darkness or alone, but your efforts will make you strong. Whatever you create, forge your relationship to the sacred Fire that transforms all things and your work will be blessed.

Magic

Make a Fire in a fireplace, a firepit, or a cauldron. Honor the wood, the charcoal, the flame. Honor your purpose. Strike a match and proclaim:

Fire, Fire, burning bright,
bringing light into the night, give me
the power of my purpose. I'll return
the gift with honor and service.

Throw your fears, doubts, and sorrows into the Fire as fuel for the life you're creating. Chant and dance. Seek visions in the flames. Tend the Fire 'til it goes out.

Goddess of Fire

Wisdom

A crimson Firebird streaks across the night sky and a feather falls. Baba Yaga, the fabled outcast, returns from wrongful banishment in a forest darkened by the broken bonds of family and tribe, bringing wisdom that is no longer handed down and shared. She stirs the Cauldron, reconnects what has been sundered, makes the magic that nurtures and protects, and tells the stories from which we learn our history. She is the Firekeeper, the giver of comfort and joy. Honor Her wisdom and Her role, for without Her, power can destroy.

Essence

Beware the mob. Seek truth. Honor the Crone. Learn the old ways.

Counsel

Who is the grandmother in your life? An older woman? Or is it you or a part of you? Respect and attend to her wisdom and the power in all she's learned—how life challenges and changes you, what matters and what doesn't, how to love and be loved. Learn the unexpected magic of how things get better with age.

Magic

Make a sacred Fire of five woods: rowan, elder, willow, hazel, and oak. Put the oak on last. Chant:

> *Fire bright, Fire burn, make the mill of magic turn! Grant the power to discern.*

Tend the ancient Fire 'til its embers glow. Tend the embers 'til they expire. Keep some ashes and add them to your next Fire. Give thanks to Baba Yaga.

WATER

Ace of Water

~ Memory ~

Wisdom

Within a mossy hollow, beneath sheltering ferns and cascading Water, lives Grandmother Toad. You might not notice her, green and glistening like her surroundings, but listen. She sings the songs of Water's magic. Water holds the Memory of everything that has ever been and ever will be, the stories carried in your cells, in your blood, in your heart, of how to live within this precious Water-filled green hollow of Life. Water carries the message of our Oneness. Swim in the Waters of Life and feel yourself remembering.

Essence

Be fully present in your feelings—emotional, physical, instinctual.

Counsel

What do you feel? Like divine magic, the Water inside you flows through you, connecting you to all things. To work with it, you must pay attention to how your emotional and physical feelings are connected. Feel the *physical* sensations of your emotions—where and how you feel them in your body. Dive deeper and feel the older, animal senses, your instinct and intuition. Learn to recognize them and how they manifest physically. Let your emotions surface, and feel your body and life respond.

Magic: Water Blessing

Fill a glass with Water. Thank it for its blessings. Then drink it slowly. Feel its purity cleansing you. Feel your emotions moving through your body with it. Hold the glass to your heart and send love into the Water. Offer it to Mother Earth and drink some more. Thank Water for its blessings.

2 of Water

~ Harmony ~

Wisdom

Water connects all things. Two Otters, one upon the shore, the other emerging from the Water, recognize each other and draw close. Like other Water creatures, they are playful because they feel the love of the Waters in which they live. In this Harmony, it's effortless for them to fill the Waters of Life with their happiness. Round and round they swim, chasing each other, holding each other as they float. How naturally they embody joy as they take care of themselves and each other. How magically they make the Waters in which they swim, the world in which they live, better for all Life.

Essence

Be playful. Feel pleasure. Express joy. Offer small acts of kindness. Partnership.

Counsel

What you put into the Waters of Life is what you take from the Waters of Life. It can be difficult to love yourself or to love people who are indifferent, selfish, or destructive. But love has many forms—kindness, compassion, patience, decency. Begin with small acts of self-love and allow Otter to teach you to play, to swim, to live. Look into Otter's pool and see yourself.

Magic

Do something fun by yourself. Do something fun with someone else. Be kind to yourself. Be kind to someone whose behavior annoys or antagonizes you. Observe their reaction while staying in your own "pool." Feel your joy as others respond to you.

3 of Water

~ Fog ~

Wisdom

Fog covers the world, enclosing everything in a numinous space between dreaming and waking. The world shifts by a few degrees and two realities overlap and align. As the Fog swirls, a weeping willow, its roots nourished by the Waters beside and below it, appears from the mist that lingers within its branches. Drops of Water fall from its leaves to the soft green moss, where three white Ducks rest. Stillness reigns. Fog fills the space between Sun and Earth, obscuring both, but blessing all within itself. In that moment of realization, acceptance, and peace, the Fog dissolves and a distant rainbow appears.

Essence

Uncertainty. Pause. Patience, receptivity. Peace.

Counsel

There are times when Life is filled with ambiguity, confusion, and resistance. Fear of the unknown or negative expectations can take hold and you may feel lost, doubtful, stuck. Fog offers a chance for contemplation, patience, and hallowing. It may cause you to wander, but you'll realize the ground is firm beneath your feet. Let the Fog of uncertainty soften and open you to wonder and trust.

Magic

The next time it's foggy, go outside. Close your eyes. Feel the Water on your skin. Breathe it in. Open your eyes. Allow the mist to take you where you need to go—backward or forward in time, deep within, into realms of Water or its Spirit. When the Fog dispels, or fills with light, arise and go forth, cleansed of doubt or fear of the unknown.

4 of Water

~ *Beauty* ~

Wisdom

A pod of humpback Whales swims in luminous Waters. They are pausing in their great migration to drift and roll, play and sing. Listen to their music moving through the Water—melodies of loneliness and grief, love and celebration. Vast distances may lie between the Whales and yet they are connected, singing together in harmony. Hunted to near extinction, Whales are returning now to fill the world with songs so beautiful, haunting, and sad that the seas are cleansed and replenished with the tears of all who hear them.

Essence

Open your heart. Grieve. Reach out. Rejoice.

Counsel

It's impossible to live without experiencing betrayal, heartbreak, and loss. It's impossible to live without feeling. Like the Whales, your heart is large enough to feel the sorrows and the joys of the world. In the depths of grief, healing comes from renewing your connections to the natural world and other beings, to friends and family. Reach out. Let your feelings, *all* your feelings, connect you to the world. They are a source of Beauty.

Magic

Whale is a wise and compassionate being who will guide you through the currents of your feelings and show you how to live in a connected way. Invite them into your life. Journey, dream, meditate, pray, study, visit with and volunteer for Whales. Allow Whale energy to move through you. Don't be surprised if you experience a sense of enhanced telepathy, gratitude, light-heartedness, and mystery. Let Whale teach you to sing.

5 of Water

~ Consequences ~

Wisdom

A Polar Bear, magnificent, strong, fitting perfectly within the world in which she lives, rides with her cubs on floating ice across a frozen sea. But the ice is melting. The perfection in which the great white Bear has always hunted, fed, and bred has disappeared in the Water's mirror. Only bits of ice are left, and the Bear is alone and starving, the sea rising and polluted. These are the Consequences of human apathy, disconnection, and destruction. This is the future we're creating. What we put into the Waters of Life is what we take from the Waters of Life.

Essence

Warning, reckoning. Interdependence. Responsibility, right action. Urgency.

Counsel

It's natural to grieve and despair when you recognize the Consequences of our collective indifference and your own. It can be overwhelming, but you can't drown in grief—you're not useful if you do. Dive deeper, beneath the pain and hopelessness. Take responsibility for yourself and your actions and do the work that's needed *now*. Do your small but important part in cleaning the world's Water, physically and metaphysically. That will clean your heart as well.

Magic: Purification

Stop magically purifying yourself by putting your negative energies into Water. Instead, ask it to work with you. Drink it, and feel its purity cleansing and blessing you within. What leaves you can then be naturally recycled and reused by Mother Earth. Offer your love and thanks to the Water.

6 of Water

~ Diving Deep ~

Wisdom

A Cormorant plunges into a darting school of Fish. The Water, the seabird's feathers, the fishes' scales, bubbles of rising Air and unexpected light all glisten, sparkle, and move. Water is the ever-changing flow of Life. Whole worlds live within it. The messages, the stories, the lives that it holds are always moving. Water itself is always moving, swirling and changing, dissolving and creating anew. Within it, Life lives and dies and lives again—fish becoming bird, bird becoming prayer, prayer becoming manifestation, manifestation coming to life. The Waters of Life are always moving....

Essence

Dive deep. Let go, go with the flow. Unexpected change.

Counsel

You cannot redirect the river of Life. Instead, plunge in, surrender to it, dissolve in it, allow the "molecules" of your expectations, plans, and intentions to mix with the Waters flowing all around you. Let go and let your heart become a vessel of understanding. Let it hold the memories of your life, of all life. To remember, you must allow the Waters of Life to flow through you. Begin now—fill the Waters of your life with stories, before the Cormorant appears.

Magic: Self-Blessing

Fill a clear bowl with warm Water (approximately 98°F or 37°C). Add three tablespoons of salt for the past, present, and future. Stir the Water until the salt dissolves. Bless yourself with the saltwater from which Life first came. Remember you too are a vessel.

7 of Water

~ Peace ~

Wisdom

The savannah is hot and dry. A stranger would feel exposed and vulnerable here, fearful that a lion might attack or that they might die of thirst. Yet there is more than struggle and threat in this parched landscape. The Waterhole is bright and welcoming, and well-worn paths lead to it. It is a gathering place where all come to drink—great cats and gazelles, elephants and others. The Earth's wisdom prevails and her children are at Peace, neither prey nor predator. The Animal People know what we have forgotten: the Waters of Life are to be shared, not fought over.

Essence

Share precious resources. Make Peace within and with others. Relief in hard times.

Counsel

How do you deal with negative feelings? Conflict, competition, and antagonism are inevitable and, in right measure, natural. They are keenest when we feel threatened, ignored, or looked down on, or worry that there's not enough for all. But Nature has an array of counterbalancing dynamics, like interdependence, cooperation, and symbiosis. Look to these now, for Peace is as organic as predation. Making Peace—with yourself and with others—is a skill as precious and life-giving as Water in the desert.

Magic: A Peace and Protection Potion

Mix together the following: lavender (4 parts), thyme (3), vervain (2), basil (3), frankincense (1), rue (a pinch), benzoin (a pinch), jasmine oil (a few drops), and bergamot oil (a few drops). Wrap your potion in cheesecloth and soak with it in your bathwater.

8 of Water

~ Instinct ~

Wisdom

The full Moon exerts its magic. Eight baby Turtles hatch from their well-buried eggs and scuttle across the sand. Something deep within urges them out of Earth and into Water, pulls them along the path of glistening moonlight, guides them from dreaming into being. It's their magic, responding to the Moon's. It's Instinct. Which do you hear when you hold a shell to your ear—the oceans' tides rushing toward you or your own blood answering the Moon's pull? The Turtles plunge into the welcoming Water. Their adventure has begun.

Essence

Awakening. Trust your Instincts. Sense the pull of destiny. Adventure awaits.

Counsel

Listen to your Instincts, your intuition, the wisdom of your heart and your body. They know things your mind can't explain. For thousands of years, we've been taught to ignore and suppress our Instincts, to think them too dangerous to rely on. But trust the magic that's within you. It's part of your true nature, just as you are part of Nature. Allow the wildness within to hatch, to run toward whatever is drawing you. Wholeness and fulfillment await you.

Magic

At the next full Moon, put a shell to your ear and listen. Strip off your clothes, strip off the egg that's protected and enclosed you. Go into Water, whether sea or stream or shower. Feel the cold Water make your heart pound within your chest. Emerge more alive than when you entered. Pay attention to your intuition.

9 of Water

~ Leap of Faith ~

Wisdom

A pilgrimage as old as time is underway. Fresh Waters mix with salt, and Salmon recognize the roiling place of their beginning and end. They enter the wild and racing stream, leaping over boulders, up Waterfalls. The wise and brave fish who knows the impossible, does the impossible—mastering the realms of Water, Air, and mystery, defying distance and gravity, battling against the current, the bears, the birds of prey, and overcoming exhaustion and fear of transformation to return home, spawn, and die. And the magic doesn't end there, for the impossible, immortal pilgrimage continues within the sacred Waters of Life.

Essence

A daunting task. Trust, determination. Go for it! Take a Leap of Faith.

Counsel

There's strength within you that defies all logic or expectation. It's the courage of the heart that has reasons reason knows not of. You're being called to defy the odds and return to the most precious things you've known since childhood. Some things in your life will die away, but new blessings will take their place. Make your Leap of Faith.

Magic

Celts, Yakima, and other Indigenous peoples have always known the Salmon is a sacred creature of wisdom and magic. Give thanks for Life's willingness to sustain your life with its own. Prepare and share a sacred meal of Salmon or vegetables and grains. Reflect on Nature's blessings and you will see the future. What you do then is up to you.

10 of Water

~ Consecration ~

Wisdom

Verdant, humid, and embracing, the rainforest grows. Tree and Vine, Butterfly and bright-beaked Toucan, tiny Tree Frog and fearsome, holy Jaguar peer through the leaves. Rain pours from above, pools on the ground below, seeps deep into the Earth, and rises to make everything grow. The rain is full of music—songs telling stories of this magical place that makes the world better for all of Life. The rainforest is wild and full of wonder, danger and divinity, chaos and perfection. There is Life and there is death, but there is no evil. It's raining and everything is blessed.

Essence

Wonderment, flourishing, blessings. The rewards of feeling fully. Waters of Life.

Counsel

What is the song your heart is secretly singing? What is the divine magic hiding within you? There's no reason for self-doubt or fear. Step outside your comfort zone and into the magic of Creation. No matter how turbulent the Waters of Life may be, how hard the rain, muddy the river, or unknown the rainforest, remember, you're made of Water, and Water makes all things grow and flourish.

Magic

Go out in the rain. Listen. What's it saying to you? Reach out your arms and feel the Water on your skin. Stick out your tongue and drink it in. Wash your face with it. Let it bless you. Feel your heart open to all that is manifesting. Collect the rainwater in a small bowl to use in your magic later and give thanks.

Messenger of Water

Wisdom

Water carries the stories of everything that has ever been and ever will be. It carries the legends of the selkie, a seal who swims forth from the cold where the mystery dwells to drop its skin and take human form. Those who live by the sea say that deep within the Waters, where the kelp forest grows thick and green, seals and selkies swim together, and with them swims a young girl with long red hair and webbing between her fingers and toes. They say she is the child of a selkie and a human, who shapeshifts as she moves between the worlds, knowing all worlds are one and all living things have their magic.

Essence

Messages, inspiration, gentleness, innocence, movement between the worlds.

Counsel

There are messages waiting for you. To find them, listen to your heart. Reread your favorite stories. Words have the magic to open doors to other realms and other ways of being. Allow yourself to be transported, enchanted, inspired. You are the author of your own story and its hero/ine.

Magic

Learn to journey, to dream, to shapeshift. Go down to the shoreline at Midsummer and offer seven tears to the sea. Call to the selkie who is calling you. Ask what s/he wants you to know. Ask yourself: "Am I a human on the land or a selkie in the sea?" Your answer will awaken the magic of both worlds.

Witch of Water

Wisdom

The Witch of Water is a being of embodied delight, conjuring magic with shimmering foam and green seaweed, salt and Water, sparkling sunlight and the feelings that flow through her. She rises from the waves, free and fully physical, dressed only in a string of pearls and a shining star, her fish tail swishing spells into the flashing froth of holy Waters. She rides the tides of feelings that come and go, luring, guiding, and fulfilling those who plunge into the sea of their desires.

Essence

Sensuality, pleasure, depth of feeling, embodied emotions. Permission.

Counsel

Being fully open to your feelings can be a rollercoaster, a raw and sometimes challenging experience. The Water Witch can show you how to be present with all of your feelings and especially how to delight in your wild and sensual nature. She knows that Water takes the shape of its container. Ask and she will show you how to shape yourself into an iridescent vessel that joyfully contains all the Waters of Life.

Magic: Attraction Spell

Mix rose, almond, vanilla, cinnamon, and lemon oils. Add seven drops, a teaspoon of salt, and seven white chrysanthemums to a warm bath. Bathe. Feel the pleasure of being in your body. When you're ready, get out of the charged Water. Let it drain and thank the sea for receiving and aiding your magic. Offer the chrysanthemums to the Water Witch at a local body of Water.

Craftsman of Water

Wisdom

The rainmaker is the Craftsman of Water. His seed rains down on the welcoming Earth and life grows. He is a trickster, a teacher who plays the clown, who understands the dance between Life and death. He may seem foolish, but he knows Life is a fragile thread and death walks alongside every one of us. He knows the fertile joy of living in the moment and how easy it is to forget in the dryness of daily demands. He clowns to startle and awaken us. Water answers him. Clouds appear in the sky, rain falls, and laughter quenches our thirst for new life.

Essence

Masculine fertility. Useful opposition. Lighten up. Spontaneity.

Counsel

Look at the beliefs you depend on and take for granted. When the opposite of what you expect appears, or when you've "made a fool of yourself," laugh at yourself and learn something useful. Let the unexpected open you up to being fully present in your life—embodied, joyful, and immersed in your feelings and sensations, rather than detached and numbed out. Life is short. Put your phone down.

Magic

Put your underwear on backward, eat dessert first, walk backward. Learn to tell a joke, a funny story. Learn about Heyokas, Kosharios, and tricksters. Play a practical joke on someone and expect them to retaliate. Spend time with people who make you laugh. Make someone else laugh.

Goddess of Water

Wisdom

Those who seek the Goddess of Water must dive deep. Sea serpents approach and dart away, and sirens' songs flood the spiraling cochlea of your seeker's ears with names more ancient than human remembering: *Tiamat*, holy primordial genetrix; *Sedna*, whose fingers became the first seals; *Tethys*, primal font of fresh Water.... The Goddess of Water glides forward, materializing as if from a dream, a woman of Water deep within Water. Rainbow-colored light pulses through Her and life grows within Her. "The ocean is my womb," She says. As She speaks, life rushes from within Her into the womb of Water around Her.

Essence

Primordial, maternal power; womb magic. Intuitive wisdom, dreaming. Fluidity. Emotional sensitivity.

Counsel

Attend to your dreams, feelings, intuition. There is new life within you. Honor your Water nature and Nature's Water. Honor the Goddess within you and all around you. Let the new life of your Spirit take form.

Magic

Make offerings to the Goddess of Water for one lunar cycle. Create an altar with a blue cloth, shells, statues of Water Goddesses, and two bowls of Water: the larger salt, the smaller fresh. Put on music, dance, and feel your emotions moving through your body. Every day, hold a cup with a small amount of Water to your heart and charge it with love, then use it to replenish the bowls on the altar. At the end of the month, offer the Waters to a body of Water near you.

EARTH

Ace of Earth

~ Healing ~

Wisdom

You cannot see her, but a woman is cradling the Earth in her arms. Look carefully. There is a pouch from which wise and magical plants are growing with primal force. The sense of anarchy and chaos is alien, yet there is a thread of familiarity, too, an ancient filament of your DNA recognizing itself, remembering its small, essential place in vast and conscious Creation. You cannot hear her, but a woman is singing to the rhythm of the medicine drum beating in her chest. Listen carefully. You can hear it beating in your own chest. Step beyond all that you have known. Step into the world. Step into Healing.

Essence

Life force, the bigger picture, humility, Healing. Mother Earth. Divine embodiment.

Counsel

You can't know who you are until you know the context in which you find yourself. Becoming healthy means letting go of self-importance and seeing yourself as a tiny part of a vast, immensely diverse, interdependent, living whole. Shift your perspective, expand your consciousness, become aware of all the beings who share this world with you. Mother Earth will teach you, guide you, heal you. Then you will know who you are and the important role you have to play.

Magic

Plant a medicine plant, like chamomile, in your garden. Tend it with love. Ask it to work with you. Harvest it with gratitude. Dry it in the Sun. Make a Healing potion with it. Return it to Mother Earth with thanks.

2 of Earth

~ Mother Bear ~

Wisdom

Here is a mystery, asleep and dreaming. Mother Bear hibernates within Mother Earth, and as she sleeps, she gives birth. Her cub sleeps beside her, and as he sleeps, he suckles. Mother Earth herself sleeps within the womb of the starry

Universe, and as she sleeps, the Great Bear in the heavens above watches over her. We live and dream between Mother Bear beneath our feet and Mother Bear above our heads. We live within the womb of Creation, being born, nursing, dreaming. In Springtime, Mother Bear stirs and awakens. Like her cub, we stretch and yawn and pad out beside her to see the beauty of the day.

Essence

Maternal blessings, beginnings, self-care, dreamtime, protection, Spirit allies.

Counsel

No matter how old you are, you are at the beginning of something new and wonderful. Look after yourself as if you were your own mother, for you are. Look after yourself as if you were your own cub, for you are. Make a commitment to your goals, set your boundaries, and have courage. Nourish your body and soul and marvel at what is emerging from you.

Magic

Stand beneath Ursa Major and give thanks. Place a Bear image, perhaps this card, on an altar and ask the Spirit of Bear to be with you. When Mother Bear appears, blessings are being offered to you by the Universe, perhaps embodied by the women in your life. Pay attention, especially to your dreams, and give thanks.

3 of Earth

~ Sacred Sight ~

Wisdom

The land is full of enchantment. Magic has been woven into it over the ages, patterns repeated over generations, but we often miss what's hiding in plain sight. The Ancestors and the Celtic Fae, the fair folk, the *Aes Sidhe*, and the *Twlyth Teg* have all played their part and are here now, among us but unseen, and in the Otherworld, which is but a step away. They are visible to those who have the eyes to see. The blue splodge in the eyes of the Horses grazing among the primroses means they see. If you ask respectfully, they may carry you to the Otherworld. How you get back is another magic.

Essence

Regaining sacred sight. Spirit beings. Magic is afoot. Step outside your comfort zone.

Counsel

In many ways you're in a comfortable place in your life, but there are important things you're not seeing. Spend time in whatever bit of Nature you can find and your own nature will be better—physically, emotionally, and spiritually. And you'll start to see the most important magic of all—the Divine is embodied.

Magic: A Folk Spell for Seeing Fairies

Eat a primrose flower. Make an offering to the fairies at a magical place—an ancient site, a hollow hill, a fairy tree (usually a hawthorn), your place of power. Be polite if you do meet them, but don't eat what they offer or you'll be trapped in their realm!

4 of Earth

~ *Standing Stones* ~

Wisdom

Four Standing Stones from long ago stand guard today. Placed in the eternal four directions, forming the square within the circle that all Witches make, they mark the union of what is known and what is mystery. This is a place of sacred ceremony where the realm of Spirit and the realm of Earth open to each other. The space within and around them is green and gold and filled with vitality so powerful the Stones sing. Magic is grounded in this land. Enter and experience how Creation is charged with divinity.

Essence

Stability, balance, grounding, connection, vital principle. Sacred ground.

Counsel

Where are you on Earth? Where are you anchored? How do you create a sense of grounding and connection with Nature? With divinity? You need a place of power, a place to cultivate a relationship with land willing to work with you, where you can receive healing, energy, and strength, and learn to give them back.

Magic: A Place of Power

Find a quiet, welcoming spot and ask Mother Earth to work with you. If you feel her agree, take four stones and place them in the four directions. Stand in the center. Send roots from your feet and spine into Mother Earth. Draw her nourishing energies into yourself. Feel the vitality and stability in this place, in yourself. Return the energy to Mother Earth with thanks. Take care of your place of power and it will take care of you.

5 of Earth

~ *One Thing Becomes Another* ~

Wisdom

A wild Hare, the Goddess's familiar, leaps above Mother Earth, over the weeds and grasses, clover and wildflowers that feed her, over her mother's bones resting in the Earth beside her newborn offspring. Life is its own circle. Life and death and new life—One Thing Becomes Another in the Mother. Nothing is wasted, nothing lost. The knife lying here is man's creation, a tool with which to harvest, but the copper from which it was fashioned was a gift from Mother Earth. All creatures know how to live, taking no more than they need and giving back in kind. When did we forget?

Essence

Life, death, and rebirth. Reduce, reuse, recycle. Don't be greedy.

Counsel

Pay attention to what you're consuming and why. Pay attention to the waste you're creating. There is no waste in Nature—everything is returned to Mother Earth to be remade. How can you express your gratitude for her gifts and give back? Begin with small steps and observe how you change. Then you change the world.

Magic

The first thing magic changes is you. Commit to finding ingredients for your spells from healthy, sustainable sources. Find local substitutes for exotic ingredients. Work with the plants and rocks that can be found where you live. Be sure to return things to Mother Earth, with thanks, when you no longer need them.

6 of Earth

~ *Dragon's Eye* ~

Wisdom

It's said that if you're willing to make the assay, to get lost and pay the cost, you'll find the Dragon's Eye and in it see the future. To some, the Dragon's Eye is a hole in a rock, carved from granite by falling rain. But when it fills with Water, it becomes a Witch's scrying bowl. Be brave, lean in, and look closely. When you do, you'll see what lies ahead. You may also awaken the sleeping Dragon. Will you risk it?

Essence

Reflect. Consider all the possibilities. Choose wisely. Unexpected challenges. Self-control.

Counsel

It's possible to see the future. Is it foolish to look? Have the courage now. You may not be able to control the events that lie ahead, but you can control how you respond to them. Here's a Witch's secret: *Do your best to face whatever life brings and you'll change your fate.*

Magic: A Dragon's Sight Potion

Carve "Sight and Insight" into a white candle. Then make a weak tea of dried yarrow and eyebright to open your sight. Let it cool, take a couple of sips, and add the rest to a bowl of Water. Place the candle behind the bowl and light it. Consecrate yourself with the Water, then look into the bowl. When you've seen all you need to, blow out the candle. Pour the potion on the Earth, then thank the Dragon. Remember the secret.

7 of Earth

~ *Running Stags* ~

Wisdom

Wild magic stampedes through the green and sacred woods, filling the forest with the sound of hooves pounding the Earth and branches breaking, and the scents of cedar and pine, oak and musk. A herd of Stags is running. The rut is on! Give way to their virile jousting, antlers crashing in combat. Though none are killed, dominance, ecstasy, and the future are won. They are a force of Nature. Catch a glimpse of the seven Stags, or even one, a sign of Life's untamed and glorious potency, and be blessed.

Essence

Masculine, animal energies; fertility, vitality, strength, sexuality. *Carpe diem*!

Counsel

Regardless of your gender, within you is an untamed animal power, a divine blessing of masculine vitality and sexuality, instinctual creativity, and strength that can be harnessed if you have the courage to be open. Channel that strength and drive. You need the animal part of yourself to sense, appreciate, and enjoy the magic and divinity of your body. Here is the power to create the life you've always longed for. Seize it!

Magic

Go out in the woods and call in the divine wildness and animal power of Creation with the words:

Hoof and horn, hoof and horn,
all the dies shall be reborn!

Call from the wildness in your heart. The Horned God will hear you. He will guide you in the wild hunt for your embodied Spirit. But be prepared to be changed.

8 of Earth

~ Spirit of Place ~

Wisdom

Slowly walk a patch of land in a garden, field, or wood. Take off your shoes, bend down, and touch the green grass, the cold stone, the bare soil beneath your feet. Look carefully. It takes time to know every rock and pebble, every leaf and twig, to know the ground beneath your feet. Wherever you are, around you are guardian olive, pine, or oak, their intertwining roots and branches encircling you with magic. You stand between the worlds, where the worlds are One. There's a Spirit of this Place, a *genius loci*. Look and listen. It will come to you.

Essence

Go outside. Know where you are. Pay attention. Spirits of the land. Humility.

Counsel

Are you seeing what's in front of your nose? It's hard to see your true, natural, and sacred self in the midst of a culture that thinks the Divine is somewhere else. But it's as close as your next breath, your next walk in the woods. Nature is your best spiritual teacher. It will show you that Creation embodies divinity, and so do you.

Magic

Wherever you are, there's a Spirit of Place. Journey, meditate, use grounding and guided visualization to meet that Spirit. It may appear as an animal or plant, a mythic being or person. Ask what it needs and do what it asks. Welcome the beginning of a beautiful, magical, and deeply healing relationship for you both.

9 of Earth
~ *Wolfpack* ~

Wisdom

The Wolfpack moves silently across the frozen tundra. High above, the *aurora borealis* blazes across the night sky with impossible magic. The Wolves have their own impossible magic. They are navigating across the snowy plain without path, landmark, or monument. They know the Earth so well they can read the subtle signals—the ice beneath their paws, the wind on their fur, the Earth's electromagnetic fields in their bones, the Sun or stars above—and know where these all lead. They know exactly where they are going because they know exactly who they are. They are arctic Wolves.

Essence

Instinct, honesty, integrity. Listen to your body. Know and accept yourself.

Counsel

Who are you? What are your motives, your intentions, your inhibitions? When you're honest with yourself and know exactly who you are, without judgment, then you know where you stand. This is essential to integrity. Call on the support and insight of friends and family who know and love you just the way you are. Accept yourself and where you are in your life and you can find your way to anywhere.

Magic: Call Wolf to Guide You

Cultivate silence while walking in Nature to create space for the Spirit of Wolf to appear. Pay attention to subtle signs in the landscape of your life and trust your intuition. Wolf will help you find your way to your true self and your destiny.

10 of Earth

~ *Web of Life* ~

Wisdom

Seize the golden thread leading into the magic forest, a strand in the Web of Mushrooms and Mycelium, the conscious Web of Life. Lie upon the mossy ground and listen. Below the surface of soil and perception is a network of connection, alive and humming with messages, pulsing with the energy, nourishment, and healing flowing from one being to another. Everything is joined in this interwoven mystery, this hidden world within the world. It seems strange and other, yet familiar and ecstatic when you taste it on your tongue. Your DNA will recognize what your mind has forgotten: all beings are connected and depend upon one another.

Essence

Consciousness of Creation, interconnection, communion, green wisdom. You are never alone. Web of support.

Counsel

You're called into deeper community and higher consciousness, beyond your current understanding. The Plant People are willing and wise teachers, and many are healers who will teach you about the medicine within the heart of every person. Commit to a path of beauty, harmony, and balance in body and soul. Recognize, revere, and celebrate your connections with Creation.

Magic

Take a walk. Ask a plant to be your ally and teacher, to help you understand the greater consciousness of Life. It may be a weed growing in a sidewalk crack or the largest tree in the park. Whatever it is, observe it, listen to it, talk to it. Research its biology, folklore, and medicine. Cultivate your relationship with it and honor its wisdom.

Messenger of Earth

Wisdom

The Reindeer Seer, the Messenger of Earth, stands beside her beloved companion and guide. Their world is snow-covered and painted with blue shadows cast by the distant Sun. The Seer is young to have the gift of sight. But it's because she is young that she is able to see the future clearly. Civilization has not tied the blindfold of distraction and conformity over her eyes. Her gift is a heavy burden, but she sees it's possible to shape the future. She will say what she sees. Will the world listen?

Essence

Foresight, weighty responsibility, incorruptibility, virtue. Possibility. Honesty. Truth.

Counsel

Whether visions come through natural intuition or skillful divination, you can see the future. Don't be afraid that it can't be changed. Witches know that fate is what you make it. Not everything is within your control, but if you use your power to control yourself, the future *will* be yours to shape. Look within and see what you can change now in order to change what will be. Then look around and see the future is not just about you. The world needs her Witches.

Magic

Do another reading and ask the Reindeer Seer to show you what you need to heal in yourself and in the world. Then begin. Commit to doing one small thing for yourself that is connected to doing something for Mother Earth. And follow through. When a Witch gives her word, she must keep it.

Witch of Earth

Wisdom

"I am the oldest," the Earth Witch says. Shapeshifter, shaman, fearsome she stands, guarding the entrance to a sacred place that is everyplace to those who see. No one may pass who is not ready to be in service to Mother Earth. Draw closer if you dare, but to cross the threshold you must be like the Witch—fierce and compassionate, courageous and humble. Will you make the commitment she demands? In the face of danger, will you help her safeguard the future of Life itself?

Essence

Challenge, service, purpose, commitment, courage. Prepare for battle.

Counsel

You're being called to serve something greater than yourself, something that will make you greater than you are. Service to Mother Earth will give you purpose and courage. It will give you magic. It will give you and the Earth healing. Some skills are instinctual, others have to be learned. The wisest teacher is Mother Earth herself. Approach the Earth Witch with respect and learn how to work with the divine power you embody.

Magic: A Bear's Heart Potion

For courage under pressure, first create a Bear altar. Then mix together ground bayberry, ground buckeye, one bay leaf, some basil, five datura seeds, and three drops of honey or a piece of honeycomb. Add a stone and a bit of Earth from your place of power. Put it all in a small leather pouch. Charge it on your Bear altar. Carry it when you need Bear magic.

Craftsman of Earth

Wisdom

There's a wild and uncontrollable presence in the greenwood, in every garden, forest, and field, and beneath all the concrete of all the cities of the world. It's primordial and vital, cleaving and engulfing every obstacle with its green and growing power. Flower and fruit burst forth as civilizations crumble and disappear. Amid the rampant greenery, a face appears—it's the Craftsman of Earth, the Green Man. Surrender to his life-sustaining power and a verdant blessing will be yours.

Essence

Creative chaos. Joy and hope in letting go. Fertility, life force, green magic.

Counsel

Without wild growth, your Spirit will lack its full power to manifest. You need to let go of some of that control you've been taught is necessary. Get outside. Feel the rush of Nature's power. Experience the wild, chaotic life force that your soul needs to grow. Pay attention to what the Plant People have to teach you. Embrace and embody your green, growing, and natural Spirit.

Magic

Approach a wildly overgrown thicket or hedgerow and ask it if it will teach you. If it agrees, step close, place your hands on the brambles and leaves, and feel their smooth and welcoming, sharp and dangerous textures. Ground yourself. Feel the energy flowing through the plants, through you. Feel the wild green Spirit within you growing. Feel its joy and hope. Thank the Green Man.

Goddess of Earth

Wisdom

When Summer comes, lie down with your belly to Mother Earth's belly. Smell the soil, the scent of life being nourished. A woman, a cow, an ancient figure of strange and welcoming wonder, appears. Barley to Her East, blue lotus to Her West, She stands before you, Her milk filling the bowl in Her lap and overflowing, spilling into a river running through the green valleys around Her. She wears the crown of blessings, a bee skep, between Her horns. Honey drips between Her gentle eyes. She is milk and honey. She is the land. She nurtures us from Her body. How She loves us! Let Her mark your forehead, and your mind will open to the stars.

Essence

Maternal blessings, love, nourishment, abundance. Divine Love embodied. Gratitude. Sweetness of Life. Encouragement.

Counsel

The Earth Goddess, Mother Earth, appears to bless you with the nourishment your body and soul need. She embodies love and abundance. Hers is the real Law of Abundance: one seed, planted, tended, and harvested, yields a thousand. But you must also know the real secret: *Take no more than you need, give back in kind, and there will always be enough for everyone.*

Magic

Create an outside altar for the Earth Goddess with offerings of food and Water, milk and honey for Her and Her other children in whose midst you live. Express your gratitude for the blessings, nourishment, and encouragement She offers you. Then you may ask for help in creating more abundance in your own life.

THE MAJOR ARCANA

1 (XXI) World

Wisdom

The World is on Fire. The time of ancestral prophecy, of dismemberment, of unmaking, is here. Civilizations and their illusions of separation and control are coming to an end. Mother Earth cannot be dominated. The Goddess is rising to protect Her endangered children.

Grandmother Spider weaves the web of the Universe, and the Goddess Kali wields the sickle knife, destroying the destroyers of Life. But in her other hand, Kali holds the spindle from which Grandmother Spider weaves. Together they tear and mend, unmaking to repair and make again. You cannot see them, but you can see their magic everywhere.

It's all One, and this is where it begins.

Beyond the blazing towers and deadly heat waits the World as it is meant to be—holy, green, and summoning. There are those who respond to the call from that World, from what lives beyond human limitations. By coincidence, by choice, and by sacred ways, they journey to discover their way home.

A young woman, her gaze fixed on the ground before her, hat pulled low upon her brow and heavy pack on her shoulders, walks alone. She carries the weight of the old World with her, remnants of what she has been taught to believe about the World and about herself. She has been bound by constraints and limits, and she longs for a better way to live. She knows there's another World within her, another World awaiting her.

She has broken free. She strides into the unknown. Her pilgrimage has begun.

Essence

Prophecy. End of illusions and domination. Breaking free. Determination. A choice that changes everything.

Counsel

The journey to sovereignty, self, and wholeness requires leaving limiting patterns and beliefs behind. You may start out frightened, burdened, and alone, but you'll discover wise and loving companions, guides, and Spirits along the path to your true self. Challenges will make you stronger, wiser, and more loving, and countless more blessings await you. It's time to discover where you are in your life, who you are, and why you're here. All that you were meant to be is ready to be born.

Magic

There's something you've been taught to believe that limits what you know to be true—about yourself, about life, about the World. Write down this constraining belief. Then take a white candle and carve the word "Truth" into it. Light it and burn the paper. Write down something good that you know to be true. Hold it behind the candle and let the light of truth shine upon it. Take time to envision the good that you've written. Remember that words are magic. Keep your magic someplace safe and look at it often.

2 (XX) Initiation

Wisdom

There's an ancient path for becoming human, for finding freedom and our own selves; there's a way to heal and to become whole, to discover who we are, where we are, and why we're here. From the moment of our first awakening, we have created rites of revelation, Initiations into the Mysteries hiding in plain sight.

Isis and Osiris, Persephone and Demeter, Inanna, Dionysus, Odin, and Mother Earth herself have cleared the path before us. A single stalk of wheat, a flower, a grape—the wisdom was once held aloft to guide us. But we shrouded it in secrecy and symbols, then forgot their meaning. We forgot the way. And yet it's still there. The path is as unique as she who walks it, but it leads through the same sacred landscape to the same destination as ever. It leads home.

Trees stir and breathe. Birds sing in their branches as the leaves rustle and dance. The Pilgrim kneels beside a stream to drink, washes her face, sees herself reflected in the Water cupped in her hands. A sign of her quest hangs from her neck, five seed-shaped spaces waiting to be filled. A Crow plucks off her hat, two Fox cubs play and tear at her pack, a Badger carries her past away.

The path leads down, deep beneath the surface, and inward to the very center of her soul. Those who are becoming wise willingly descend, ready to be unmade in order to be made again. It's time for unburdening, for cleansing the unreal and unwanted, for shedding all that separates you from your sacred self, from the Sacred that surrounds, sustains, and summons you. It's time to die and be reborn.

Trusting what guides her, the Pilgrim prepares herself. She knows the time will come to rise and return, carrying the magic and the gold she has discovered, knowing that she is loved and protected by the Source from which she first arose.

Essence

Purification. Initiation. Trust. Let go of the past. Go within. Plunge into the unknown.

Counsel

What's behind you? What are you carrying with you? What do you need to unpack? To leave behind? Life will initiate you, and when that journey begins, you must be ready to confront the emptiness of a socially dictated life and the constraints of family conditioning. You must face your fears and self-doubts, your shadows and your "dark" side. You must release what imprisons you. It's difficult, but it's joyful. It begins with a single step, a leap of faith that although the old will fall away, something new, true, and beautiful will take its place. Plunge into the Water, into the cave. Plunge into your life. Everything will teach you, once you are open.

Magic

Fill a tub with warm Water and sprinkle in fennel, anise seed, and dandelion—flower, stem, and leaves. Step in. Hold your breath and plunge beneath the surface. Submerge yourself. Feel the magic happen, sit up, head out of the Water, and breathe. Relax and let the old and outworn dissolve. Thank the Water. When you're ready, step out and know your life is beginning anew.

3 (XIX) Sun

Wisdom

There's a divine light that shines even in the darkest of times, when you face the most hidden and shameful things within you, when you are confronted by the most flagrant and wounding things in the world around you.

The young Hawk God Horus descends with the Sun in his beak, offering it to you. Like a baby bird, open your mouth and swallow it. The Sun now shines within you, so you can see what you must. Slowly, organically, magically, the time has come to accept and love the most hidden, most wounded things about yourself, the things you feel ashamed of, the things you hide away.

A sacred spark stirs. A Fire ignites, warming and transforming, and, as surely as the Sun rises in the morning, the magic of healing and renewal follows. The first thing the Sun's magic brings to life is you.

The Pilgrim's heart beats again and joy awakens within. He finds the courage to hold his heart and his shame, his brokenness and his beauty, for all the world to see. He is serene and radiant, surrounded by allies who are helping him transform wounds into wisdom, humiliation into hope, emptiness into splendor.

Life begins again, sustained by the Sun.

Essence

Seeing what was hidden. Vulnerability. Self-awareness, self-respect, healing, triumph Energy.

Counsel

Look at what most frightens, shames, and wounds you. With time, patience, and tenderness, you'll learn to accept, forgive, and love yourself. You'll figure out the lessons to be learned and, as if you're turning a key in the lock of your past, your patterns will break open. You'll earn your own self-respect. A spark of new life will stir within you, and healing and joy will follow. And when you're ready to share what you're most afraid of letting the world see, your courageous vulnerability will become the Sun for others who are seeking the light of healing and transformation. When you heal, the world heals.

Magic

Choose a day to rise with the Sun. Go outside and greet it. Lift your arms and reach out to its returning light. Offer it your sadness, your sorrow, your woundedness, and feel your pain transforming. Let it be seized by Hawk and carried off to feed the Fire and make it burn more brightly. Grasp the Sun in your hands and bring it into your heart, into the space left by the pain you offered up. Feel its warmth and light, power and joy, glowing within you. Place your hand over your heart during the day and feel the Sun shining within you, healing all your wounds. When you're ready, you may wish to share the story of your sadness with someone you love and trust.

4 (XVIII) Moon

Wisdom

There's a wildness within us that yearns to be physical, sensual, animal, free. But fear of this unknown part, of the shadows where it dwells, of where it might take us and who it might make us, has left us all only half alive.

We live in a human world of comfort and possessions, safe and secure but cut off from the natural world, from our body, from the magic of embodiment. It's the Moon that illuminates our ancient longing. When it appears in the night sky of our soul, it's a holy grail finally within reach, a cup of the wine of Life in which our dreams of wholeness float. It's the Moon that pulls us forward with its rhythmic ebb and flow, a mystery that women's bodies know. Diana, Goddess of Witches and all things wild, holds the mirror of her full and shining Moon for us to see our sacred selves, no longer hidden, doubted, or unconscious.

The Pilgrim goes to see her reflection. She enters the dark woods and Wolves appear. She slips into the deep Waters where Otters play. She even dares to brave the Dragon's lair.

Wildness is the only path to the Moon. There's no need to dread the companions who will teach you how to shapeshift into hoof and horn, paw and claw, fur and feathers, fins and scales, bud and leaf and flower. Set your foot upon the silver path. The Moon will light your way from fear to the fierce and freeing desires of your wild and natural self.

Essence

Mystery. Wildness, physical instinct. Liberated feminine power.

Counsel

When the Moon appears and the wild calls, what will you choose? The illusory safety of your city tower? The sanctuary of a Witch's cottage with its tiny light shining in the forest? You can't pretend that's wildness. Howl at the Moon. Race with Wolves, swim with Otters, fly with Owls. Look back into the far distance and see the light from your cottage window. Feel a pang of sorrow for all that you have let go. Then turn to the Moon above and feel a shiver of delight as you hear the answering howl of your companions. Watch the Moon, follow its rhythm in the sky, see how it pulls the tides below. Feel that pull within you, rising and subsiding. Feel the Moon in your body, in your heart, in your mind. When you choose to return to your cottage and community, you'll return changed—free, whole, and holy, blessed by the Moon.

Magic

At the next full Moon, take a small round mirror and go outside. Capture the Moon's reflection in the mirror. Now look at yourself in it. See the light in your eyes, even in the darkness. Tilt the mirror until you can again see the shining Moon. Look at yourself again. See yourself more clearly. See the light that shines within you, see the magic that shines within you, see the future that awaits you. Lift the mirror to the Moon and give thanks for the blessing She has given you.

5 (XVII) Star

Wisdom

There's a light within you that shines in your eyes when you're awake and aware. It's the magic of your purpose, held aloft to light the path before you. But until you know who you are, you won't know where you're going. Shining with the essence of your being, your joy, your destiny, it's time to be guided by a gleaming and heavenly radiance, reminded that you're such stuff as Stars are made of. Dive deep and you will remember why you're here.

The Pilgrim ventures through night and woods and wildness, unafraid of the unknown. The path abruptly ends before a pool as black as a scrying mirror. She looks in but sees no reflection, just her shadow, and then the Water clears, filling with countless points of light. Stripping off her clothes, she slips into the magic, lies back, and floats, gazing up at the Stars that float above her, suspended amid the Stars that float around her.

The Pilgrim seeks the brightest one, the true North of her own becoming. Just beyond her grasp, it pulls her toward her dreams. She dives deep into peace and beauty beyond all imagining. As joyful as an Otter playing, determined as a Salmon leaping, supple as a Seal swimming, she is one with the luminous Waters.

Joyous and buoyant, she bursts up from the shimmering depths and climbs ashore, dripping with Water and starlight. The sky fills with shooting Stars and she cups her hands together and reaches up. A Star falls into her palms. She holds it close for a moment, then brings her offering down to the Earth. Water and starlight spill from her hands.

The Pilgrim looks into the pool and sees herself. She is the Star.

Essence

Sacred signs. Illumination, inspiration, insight. Purpose. Destiny. A blessing received.

Counsel

You are the manifestation of Creation's magic. You are a love spell cast by the Divine to bring beauty, life, and love into the world. It can be hard to believe and easy to forget. You may feel panic that the vision you're carrying, your goals, and your ambitions will become a heavy yoke around your shoulders, a burden that you're not up to carrying. You're making it heavy because of doubt and worry. Remember, Stars are light.... Learn to carry your purpose with joy and then it won't be so weighty. It's time to make the offering of your starlight, the essence of your being, your heart, your bliss, the reason why you're here. The

Star is a sign that you're on your path. You have a purpose, a gift, a blessing to offer that will make the world a better place for your having been here. This is what it means to be a Star.

Magic

Go outside and make a wish upon the first Star you see. Dance beneath your Star and feel your power to make your wishes come true. Write it all down when you get home, and the next day, take a step toward making your wish come true. Continue making your starlit magic and taking action until your magic manifests.

6 (XVI) Maze

Wisdom

On the Pilgrim's back remains the pack, but it's smaller now. How far he's come by stepping off the path he knows, by getting lost and tumbling downward, confused, disoriented, and exhilarated. There have been blessings on the way, gold and silver and stars in the darkness. But twists and turns lie ahead. The great unmaking has just begun, the old ways are still to be undone.

Magic waits within the Maze. The Pilgrim stands poised upon its edge. The moment of choosing has arrived as his guide slips out of sight. Who calls from deep within? Who dwells in the center of the Maze? Demon or divinity? Minotaur, monster, or source of Love and Life? The old self or the new?

A sense of panic rises, for when you don't know where you're going, which way do you go? Without bearings, you could be lost forever.

A lightning bolt strikes, cleaving the darkness for a flashing instant, dangerous but revealing.

The mystery has an ancient pattern: you must die to be reborn, releasing the past for the future to take form. The Pilgrim enters the Maze, trusting the unknown and knowing that there is no turning outward until the self within is found.

Essence

Inhibitions, disruption, uncertainty. Risk-taking. Let go. Be here now.

Counsel

Stop trying to make a plan, or choose a path, or do anything other than just be. Relinquish control. Let go of all your carefully constructed plans, your thoughts about what comes next. Let go of the road map. Let go of the safety of your conscious mind. The unmaking and remaking will continue at a deeper level, and you can't force or rush or push the process, you have to let it happen. Trust that something else, something sacred, will guide you to where you're meant to be and who you're meant to become. Be present in the moment. That's where the magic is happening.

Magic

Do the opposite of something you have carefully planned. Say "no" when you feel you must say "yes." Go outside when you want to stay in, especially if it's raining or snowing. Help someone you don't know. Give something away. Take in a stray. Get to know the you that's been hiding away.

7 (XV) Ancestor

Wisdom

How many silver threads connect you to Life? They emerge from your heart, an unfurling path full of promises that shimmers like a mirage of the future then fades from view. Is the Pilgrim's quest for her true purpose merely an illusion? Has she come to an *impasse* imposed by an unseen past or has she found the wisdom way forward?

Cobwebs bind the Pilgrim to those who have gone before her. Grandmother, grandfather, generations long gone haunt and pull, whisper and advise. Stories of the past live in the present and forecast the future. The Pilgrim's path spirals forward then circles back, marked with drops of blood drawn by the sharp thorns of ancestral patterns. Each generation inherits the wounds of their lineage, has their dreams confined by conditioning, finds their desires entangled in roses planted long ago that pierce and prick but also perfume the Air with promise and potential.

The Pilgrim appeals to Hekate Phosphoros, Goddess and guide through the Underworld. She offers prayers to the Ancestors to guide her through the darkness and to the gold. An Ancestor hears and responds, for she knows the magic and will joyfully share it. There's a blessing in the family curse. The burning torch is held aloft. The shining key to the ancient dungeon is inside the cell. The Pilgrim lifts it from its place and honors her forebears. They are the reason she is here. The door swings open, the path appears, and she emerges, bringing treasure to the world.

The Ancestor gives her blessing:

> *The past is not a burden; it is the gift of those who have gone before and brought you to this day. Accept their blessing and forgive the rest. You are free to be who you are meant to be and to create your own life. Make your magic.*

Essence

Family, continuity, inheritance, patterns. Past trauma, forgiveness, gratitude. Ancestral blessings.

Counsel

The Ancestor appears to pose the question: "Why are you here?" Perhaps you've just been passing time and letting life pass you by. It's time to ask yourself: "Which way do I want to go from here?" If you ask the Ancestor for advice, she will tap her chest and say: "You have to follow your heart." And then she will tap her head and remind you: "Too much following this. It might make the way easier, but it won't make you happy."

Reflect on the choices you've made. See the unconscious patterns of childhood, the ways of coping with the traumas and sorrows you inherited from your parents, who inherited them from theirs. See that all thorns protect roses. See the secret gifts you've inherited and the powers you've cultivated that will serve your unique purpose now. It is time to follow your inner compass through life. No one can tell you which way to go and no one can stop you from finding your own way. So, go forward. Trust your heart.

Magic

This magic is best done at Samhain, 31 October. Create an ancestral altar. Decorate it with seasonal flowers, fruit, other things of beauty. In the center, place pictures of your Ancestors—grandmothers, grandfathers, parents, relatives who have gone before you and crossed over. Light a yellow candle and study their faces. Reflect on their sorrows and their successes. Write down their stories and what they taught you, good and bad. Thank them for both, forgive them, and honor them. Forgive and honor yourself. Blow out the candle and keep the pictures safe.

8 (XIV) Healing

Wisdom

Follow your heart. The Pilgrim follows hers, along mossy banks, beside tumbling Waters, by hedgerows filled with singing birds, through long greenwood tunnels, and along windy cliffs above seaside villages. The path passes through tall grasses and wild weeds that lay gentle but unrelenting siege to the statues that once pointed the way, old idols of human pride, projection, and power. What is not growing is dying, and so the Pilgrim strikes off into the unmarked undergrowth toward the wildwood, plunging into Life.

Blackthorn scratches her as she brushes past and she begins to feel poison spreading through her. A fever burns and, dizzy, she lies down in meadowsweet and yarrow. She looks into the heavens above as the Yarrow People encircle her and brush her with their petals. Pollen falls on her. Unseen but ever-present, the Goddess Brigid sings her Healing enchantments and wraps the Pilgrim in a curing cloak of sleep. Old wounds open and empty as she floats in slumber deep.

It's said that losing love leaves a hole in your heart so large you will hear the wind blow through it, but in time you'll grow a larger heart around the hole. The Pilgrim drifts up through the hole in her heart to the dusky indigo sky above. Ancestors encircle her, looking down from the Otherworld, murmuring softly with the Yarrow.

She floats between the worlds....

Rooted firmly in Mother Earth, the Plant People know that we're deeply wounded, suffering from delusions of separation and superiority. We have so much to learn. Ask for help and you'll feel them weaving their mending magic around your broken heart. Look and you'll see them as our equals—conscious, compassionate, and wise. Pay attention. They are sharing the breath of Life and its magic with you. It's time to heal.

The Pilgrim wakes and sits up. She is hungry, thirsty, and covered in pollen.

Essence

Wounding. Rest, patience, Healing, resilience. Green magic. Empathy.

Counsel

When least expected, wounding occurs, or reoccurs. You're not invincible; you aren't meant to be. Wise ones know that you cannot heal the wounds of others until you've healed your own. And Healing takes time. This is a time of waiting, of stillness, non-action, and reflection, of rest and rehabilitation. When you're ready, you'll realize that your wounds have opened you to compassionate connection to Life. This connection will heal you and you'll become a healer who knows the pathways of empathy, kindness, and resilience. Remember why you're here and you'll be at peace. Patience....

Magic

Consider a wound within that needs Healing. Write about it with compassion. What advice would you give a friend who came to you with this concern? Turn to a friend and ask for their help. Then ask for help from the Plant People: wrap a Healing potion of yarrow, meadowsweet, and chamomile in a small square of white cotton cloth. Tie it up with three knots in a blue ribbon, and as you do so, chant:

Feeling, feeling, feeling. It is love,
love, love that is Healing, Healing,
Healing. All the past sorrows are
the strength of my tomorrows.

Press the pouch to your heart and keep it with you. Be patient and be kind to yourself. When you're ready, open it and return the herbs to Mother Earth, with thanks for their help and hers.

9 (XIII) Rebirth

Wisdom

The Sun has gone into the seed. Life has outgrown itself and the sickle falls, separating our past from our purpose. When wisdom is the harvest, nothing is wasted. The Pilgrim learns an ancient magic: a single stalk of wheat held aloft is a sign that all that falls shall rise again. Her soul work continues deep beneath the surface, where a single seed contains a thousand more.

Dreams of a new life stir and rise. Holding fast to her hopes, the Pilgrim is reborn. She is mastering the magic of the Green God Osiris, eternally cut down, interred, and returned to Life with incantations of Love. She is mastering the magic of Dionysus, Inanna, and Persephone, and of Mother Earth, whose eternal blessing is Rebirth.

Life leaps forward with her—flowers blooming, birds singing, animals playing, Spirit allies appearing, as the Pilgrim dances to the song of Creation, to the beat of her heart, to the rhythm of returning and rejoicing. She dances, one foot in the center and on the ground, the other on the edge of the circle spinning her round. She dances, knowing that the form of Life changes, but the energy of Spirit is eternal.

This is the turning point in every Pilgrim's journey. The Pilgrim is becoming a *wicce*, a wise one, seeing the Sacred within and around her. She sees eternal Spirit outside time and embodied Spirit within time. She has reached the ending of non-being. Unmaking is turning into making. She is ready to create her life, her dreams, her purpose.

We are Stardust illuminating the world as we walk. We are Life embodying Spirit as we walk. We are dust and Water walking, chanting the spell of living well.

Essence

Turning point, new start. Exhilaration. Resurgence. Return. Springtime. Hope fulfilled.

Counsel

It can be difficult to let go of the past, or dreams that haven't come true, or love that is no longer in our life. But Creation teaches that every ending is followed by a beginning. Nothing in life, no matter how painful or challenging, is wasted when you exercise the magic of discernment. Ask yourself: "What purpose did this event in my life serve? Why did I make the choices I made? What can I learn from what I've gone through?" Find the answers and everything changes. There's meaning and purpose in every challenge, loss, or sorrow, if you put it to use. When you find the meaning, you'll find yourself able to begin again, wiser, stronger, and better than before. The energy of Life will flow through you and what once seemed impossible will be within reach. Trust that when the time is right, you'll arise, revitalized and ready.

Magic

This is magic best done in the Spring. Take a small flowerpot outside, along with a packet of zinnia seeds and some Water. Fill the pot with Earth and hold it in one hand and the seeds in the other. Pick one important goal and focus on it. Plant a few seeds in the soil. Hold the pot up to the Sun and down to the Earth. Water the seeds and chant:

Hopes and plans, seeds and grain,
all that falls shall rise again.

Send your energy into the planted seeds. Take good care of them, giving them Sun and Water and love, and take action to manifest your magic. (When the flowers fade, harvest the seeds to plant again next Spring.)

10 (XII) Offering

Wisdom

Shedding the skin he has outgrown, the Pilgrim sees the unfolding mystery as his own. Vulnerability has made him strong. As he walks forward, Spirits of love and compassion make themselves known. How tenderly they speak of the sweetness of Life. The Fay Folk and the *Fata*, the *Landvaettir* and the *Aes Sidhe*, the elementals and the devas, the people of peace and the hidden people appear to share the wisdom he's forgotten.

A tall and slender Fairy, a Spirit of the land, takes the Pilgrim by the hand and invites him to go along with her. Happy to do so, he realizes this Fairy makes mending magic. Through the woods they walk, on a vast and shimmering web, their footsteps sending tiny ripples across the threads. The Pilgrim is like a newborn fawn learning how to walk, but he is human, and so he wonders what would happen if he stepped out of the pattern.

"Trust," says the Fairy.

Recognizing the wise design the world reveals and sensing that all will be well, the Pilgrim walks softly on. The web stretches deep within and high above, but all paths lead to the center, where the Tree of Life grows—roots, branches, and web interwoven as a shimmering sphere within which all reside and thrive. It's here that the song of Life was first sung. The Pilgrim listens and hears the secret magic: "I demand no sacrifice, for I am the Mother of Life and my love is poured out upon the Earth."

Like the Pilgrim, the Tree is a young being that requires nourishment, care, and the energy that makes everything grow and flourish, the energy that is embodied and exchanged by all of Creation, the energy of Love. The song continues and the Pilgrim listens to the enchantment long forgotten but no longer hidden: *All things grow and thrive and make the world a better place for Life.*

In the way of his Ancestors, with reverence and rejoicing, the Pilgrim pours out his heart. He gives back with gratitude for all the blessings he's been given.

Offer love to Mother Earth and love is given back to you. This is the wisdom and the way of Offerings.

Essence

Spirit guides. Divine patterns of connection. Love. Gratitude, giving back. Flourishing.

Counsel

Who do you love? What do you love? What do you love to do? Give yourself openheartedly to yourself, to your purpose, to those you love, and you'll flourish and so will all to whom you give your love. Give your love to the world, and the world flourishes. It's the energy of Life that makes things grow, and Life is always growing, always giving itself to more Life. Look at your choices—do they benefit only you? What are the consequences for others? Can you make a choice that benefits you without harming others, or Mother Earth? What you choose matters; what you do makes a difference. If you offer your joy and love, gratitude and generosity to Life, that is what Life will offer you.

Magic: Count Your Blessings

Consider all that you've been given. Each day for a week, write down one thing for which you're grateful. For each gift that you've received, choose a way to give back with gratitude. Do something kind and generous for someone. Find ways of giving back to Mother Earth. Whatever you choose as your Offering, do it with fullness of Spirit and heart. Watch your life flourish.

11 (XI) Balance

Wisdom

Within the magic woods, time shifts and the Pilgrim returns to her childhood. She enters the realms of Spirit and sees the world as it's meant to be. Her grandmother shows her how all things live in Balance. She points to Bear and Fox, to Rose-breasted Grosbeak and Squirrel, to mushrooms and elderberries, to passing clouds and warming Sun, tumbling stream and swimming Fish, all in perfect relationship. They teach the young Pilgrim right from wrong and how to be fair, to treat all with respect and reciprocity.

Her heart skips a beat as she remembers the future without her grandmother and wonders who teaches people then. "Mother Earth teaches all who pay attention," grandmother replies. "Remember the story I told you about the Goddess Maat? She holds a single feather to weigh against your heart. Lightness of being is the gift of balance."

Mother Earth is always teaching you what all her children know—the life-sustaining Balance that all Creation shows. Live lightly on the land. Take no more than you need and give back with gratitude for all that you've received. If nothing is wasted, there's enough for everyone.

Receiving and replenishing, interchanging and exchanging, with gratitude and generosity, perfect Balance is maintained and lightness of being is attained. Joy is what it feels like.

Essence

Choices. Prosperity, generosity. Reciprocity, equilibrium, harmony. Lightness of Spirit, joy. Energy flowing.

Counsel

Finding Balance within yourself is a key to your sense of peace, happiness, and lightness of Spirit. It's time to consider the choices you're making about your life, your time, your energy. Where do you need to pay more attention to achieve a healthy Balance in your life? How can you make changes and create more of what you need in order to be Balanced? What are your priorities? Are they making you happy? How can you Balance work with the rest of your life? Are your relationships reciprocal—do you receive as much as you give? Are you valued by those you value? Reflect on how much you have to be grateful for, how much you're given by Mother Earth, and find ways to give back, to restore Balance, inside and out.

Magic

Stand at the center of the circle of your life. Face the East, direction of Air. Do you think too much or not enough before you act? Are you still questioning and learning or worrying and doubting? Breathe in, quiet your mind, love yourself as you are, and thank the Plant People for giving you the breath of Life. Face South, direction of Fire (Northern Hemisphere), and reach up to the Sun. Are you scared or determined in pursuit of your purpose? What gives you joy? Feel the rush of that energy. Give thanks. Face West, direction of Water. Are you in touch with your feelings or are you suppressing them? Are you loving yourself enough or giving too much of yourself away? Say "I love you" and hug yourself. Face North and touch the Earth. Are you working too hard and not taking care of yourself? What needs healing? Thank your body and promise to take better care of yourself. Return to the East and take a deep breath. Feel how present you are.

12 (X) Wheel of Life

Wisdom

Divine magic whirls energy into embodiment. Earth and Sun, Goddess and God, Beloved and Lover dance together in eternal partnership as Love spins the Wheel of Life. Open-hearted and longing to learn the rhythm and its reasons, the energy and its seasons, the Pilgrim gives herself to joy, revolving round the sacred circle with one foot in the center and one foot on the edge.

The Pilgrim is learning the wisdom of the wild things who feel the seasonal stirrings, summonings, and blessings in their bodies and souls. In Winter, the seed of light sleeps within the darkest night and awakens in the Mother's belly, restless to return in Spring. Hope is rewarded as new Life emerges to flex and play. Halfway round the whirling Wheel, the Summer Sun blazes and Mother Earth blossoms. Bees buzz round the Midsummer cauldron, filling it with honey. Life flourishes, then nourishes, when the harvest sickle falls into Autumn's ripe abundance. The Sun strays further away each day, the leaves turn gold, and Winter arrives once again. Though death comes to all that lives, the cycle spins and Life begins again with a dream, resting deep within the Mother's womb where everything is possible. This is the magic, wisdom, and wonder of Creation.

The Pilgrim is learning about change. She sees Life being born and growing, flourishing, aging, dying, resting and returning. And so she sees the Mystery—the forms change, but the Spirit of Life is eternal.

"The Sun is in the seed, the seed is in the Earth...." The song that plays as the Wheel spins round is the magic of rebirth.

Essence

Earth magic. Embody, change, transcend, rejoice. The rhythm of Life. Energy cycles.

Counsel

When the Wheel appears, you are urged to pay attention to the meaning of the season and the rhythm of your own being. The body has its holy wisdom, its beauty, and its blessings, its reasons and its seasons, just like Mother Earth. Reflect on the seasons in your own life—the seeds you've planted, nourished, and harvested with hard work and conviction, the things that you've outgrown and need to leave behind, the dreams that you nourish that have yet to flourish. Pay attention to the rhythm of your body, your feelings, your life. Pay attention to Mother Earth's great cycles of creation, destruction, rest, and rebirth. Consider how you might shift your life to be in harmony with these great currents of energy.

Magic

Go outside, take a walk, and pay attention to what's happening in Nature. Notice what you're drawn to. Look for a natural object that calls to you. Ask it if it will teach you. Breathe deeply, hold it to your heart, and ask it to tell you what it knows and what you need to learn about the blessings of the season. Listen. Thank it for its wisdom and ask it if it will continue to work with you as a power object. If it agrees, leave something in its place to keep the balance. Take the power object with you and keep it somewhere safe. Write down and reflect on what you learned from it. How can its wisdom help you bring your own life into sync with Nature's rhythm? Make a promise to yourself to bring your life into greater harmony with Mother Earth. Remember, Witches keep their promises.

13 (IX) Shaman

Wisdom

At times, the Pilgrim's path leads through darkness, with hope held aloft like starlight in a lantern or the North Star shining in the heavens above. At times, she feels so lonely that the wind between the stars blows through her heart. But when she listens carefully, she hears upon that wind a song of Love so sweet and full of hope that she hums along and birds dance in the Air around her.

The Pilgrim is ready. The teacher appears.

The Shaman, arms encircled by feathered serpents who encircle the world, beats the rhythm of enchantment that accompanies his song. His mind opens, his heart opens, the way opens between the worlds, where neither time nor space constrain him, and he enters through a portal of reindeer skin stretched tight around a wooden frame. Blindfolded and in darkness, he drums the heartbeat of Mother Earth. He drums at the center of the circle, where all worlds meet as One. The rhythm reverberates throughout the worlds. Magic stirs into motion. The Shaman calls his guides to show the way.

The Pilgrim closes her eyes and listens to the drum. She listens to the heart of Mother Earth beating. Mind open, heart open, she sees the way opening before her and steps into the realm of Spirit. She hears the voices of all the peoples—plants and animals, Ancestors and elders, winds and Waters and minerals, Spirits and allies—and knows all these compassionate and loving beings are singing to her. She listens and learns what they know—the wisdom way of healing and becoming whole, of becoming a wise one. She hears Creation singing. She feels the rhythm of her heart beating in time with the heart of Mother Earth, with the heart of Creation.

Listen to the drum. The teacher has appeared to teach you the song of Life.

Essence

Apprenticeship, introspection, skills. Spirit guides, a teacher. Altered states, sensing the Sacred.

Counsel

On this path of becoming, it's time to find a teacher who will teach you the skills you need to discover your true self, to accomplish whatever gives you joy, to fulfill your destiny. When the Shaman appears, you are called to listen to the voice of the Sacred. To hear it, you must be willing to work in darkness, as the Shaman does. Learn to journey. Call the Spirits who have deep compassion and love for you and ask them to help you navigate through your life. Pay careful attention and be blessed by the heart of the Divine pulsing through Creation, pulsing through you. It's time to sense the Sacred, in the world and in yourself.

Magic

Take an offering and your magical journal, and head outside to a spot that calls to you. Sit on the Earth. Breathe and ground yourself. Take your time. Place your hand on the ground, on the breast of Mother Earth. Feel her warmth, her energy. Feel the pulse of her energy against the palm of your hand. Place your other hand on your heart. Feel your heart's rhythm in sync with Mother Earth's heart. Gently tap the rhythm of your heartbeat upon the Earth: *bum bump, pause, bum bump, pause....* Feel the energy of Mother Earth flowing through you, filling you, nourishing you. Feel her love filling you. Think of her countless generous blessings. Think of how she nourishes and sustains you, body *and* soul. Thank her. Make your offering.

Write about your experience in your journal. Next time, you may wish to bring a drum.

14 (VIII) Strength

Wisdom

The Pilgrim is awakening to her power. It courses through her from the ground up, sustaining and absolute. This force of Creation is an unfamiliar feeling and yet she knows it to be real and essential. It's hope fulfilled, potential recognized, and all that is right in the world, and in her. But how does she summon it? Wield it? What purpose does it serve? Until she has the answers, she can't unlock its magic.

There are challenges before her and time is growing short. For too long we have feared the force of Nature, thought it red in tooth and claw, or thought ourselves uniquely superior. Separated from the Sacred, we have become wounded, unconcerned, and cruel. We have ascended through domination—the mightiest predator of all—and now the world lies dying at our feet.

But Nature can't be conquered, nor is there need to do so. The Pilgrim's path has given her the Strength of the Goddess Artemis to heal what we have broken. She stands amid Nature's glory and knows where real Strength comes from and whom it's meant to serve: Creation's infinite expressions that teach us of their divinity, and our own.

A quiet, hidden wood mouse, a blue-winged butterfly, an owl, a cat curled in the sunlight, an oak tree in the garden, the heather on the hill all guide the Pilgrim now, and she plunges into Life. She becomes a salmon, swimming strongly upstream, then, scrambling to a wooded shore, becomes a bear, a wolf, a moose, a black crow flying through the Air. Fit, strong, and confident, she is able to call upon the elements, upon wind and flame, Earth and rain, to dance with them, become like them, draw power from them. We wield unwavering sovereignty when the Earth and our body are inseparable.

The Pilgrim steps out of the shadows and into view. Humble and open-hearted, she has become a Speaker for Mother Earth, for her children, for all the peoples who cannot speak for themselves, but who can teach us what it means to live rightly, to live as One. Her purpose is her Strength.

Essence

Challenges, courage, care. Heart path. Purpose, action, service. Empowerment.

Counsel

Life is full of challenges that can fill you with doubt and fear. Are you good enough? Smart enough? Strong enough? If you wait to feel courageous, you may never act at all. Here's the magic trick: *Act even if you feel afraid and you will become strong.* Leap, and on the other side you'll find your courage. Face the worst and it will bring out your best. You'll discover what you believe in *and* that you have power to do what's right, even if it seems to put you on the losing side. Stand strong, stand for what's right, speak from your heart. The path of the heart *is* the path of Strength. And whenever you doubt this, spend time in Nature. Let your heart open and feel yourself part of the whole Earth community that loves you, supports you, and knows what you really are: *strong.*

Magic

What do you believe in? Find that and you'll find your magic and your Strength.

15 (VII) Journey

Wisdom

All pilgrimages are Journeys into the unknown. The path disappears. There is neither map nor sign. Those who passed this way before left no mark on land or time. The Pilgrim is discovering where they are and so they are discovering who they are. The vastness of the land around them puts things into perspective. They have learned they can't depend on someone else's map if they are to have the great adventure of finding their own way, and so finding themselves. The landscape within will determine which way they choose, and as they choose, their inner domain of becoming whole and holy will change. They will be free. They *are* free. The future is theirs to create.

The energies of land and sea arise to greet the Pilgrim and their companion, a white Horse, who knows the inner course of instinct and natural harmony. If asked, he would carry the Pilgrim's weight upon his back wherever the Journey might take them, but the two walk as equals. The Pilgrim is learning to listen to their body, to their Spirit, to their senses and instincts as they walk beside the wise Horse. The Pilgrim is experiencing the way of mutual devotion and wisdom greater than their own.

Far off in the distance, ancient Herds thunder forward, following the ceaseless cycles of Sun and Earth. Their course is set by the seasons, a life-regenerating rhythm revealed by land and light. It is animal wisdom honored by our Ancestors who migrated in their company, unconstrained by human borders, trusting the vast tides of Life flowing across Mother Earth in search of green grass, fresh Water, and the future.

The Journey of Life is a pilgrimage. Some paths are well worn by the Ancestors of all the peoples, some are known only to those who travel between the worlds, and some become visible only when the light shifts and the way is revealed within. On this holy pilgrimage, each path is as unique as the one who walks it, but the landscape through which all travel—all the children of Mother Earth—is the same. It's sacred. And every path leads home.

Essence

Pilgrimage, movement, self-discovery. Trust the path. *Ithaca*.

Counsel

It's time to ask yourself: "Where am I going?" Your question will be answered with another question: "Where do you *want* to go?" This is a moment when great changes are underway, in yourself and in the world around you. You may feel uncertain about which direction to take, which choice is right, and what will bring you fulfillment. It's time to travel light, pack only what you need, and leave behind old ideas, especially ones that come from other people and their expectations. There are no mistakes, only adventures that will teach you who you are and why you are here. Learn to trust your instincts, trust your heart, and trust those who love you, especially your companion animals. And remember, the point of the Journey is not the destination. It's who you become along the way.

Magic

Face East, stretch out your arms, and turn slowly clockwise in a circle. Reach out to the Sun above you and the Earth below you. Close your eyes and turn inward. Where is it you wish to go next? Spin until your heart says, "Stop." Open your eyes and take the first step forward in the direction you've chosen. It's time to work magically with the element of that direction. Thank the Sun and Earth and continue your Journey.

16 (VI) Love

Wisdom

Read to us when we were children, fairy tales still cast their spells today. Love potions concocted out of words conjure the prince on his white horse, the princess in her tower, the rebel in his car speeding through the night, the girl on her front porch dancing in the moonlight. The path to Love is magical, the outcome never certain until we close the storybook and look behind the curtain. False starts and broken hearts, passion and projection.... Only when we're ready do we learn Love's true course and purpose, for what we long for on the outside we must first find on the inside.

But it takes more courage than a thousand battles, with all that we must risk, to remain vulnerable, present, and open to receive Life's greatest gift. The Universe senses when we're ready and sends a guide of true devotion, without conditions, in perfect Love and trust. And so the Pilgrim's guide appears, her familiar and companion in her quest for Love. Thick, soft fur beneath her fingers, warm breath upon her face, Fox is her beloved on this journey to become whole. She looks into his eyes and sees he's part of her soul. He looks into her eyes and sees she is part of his. From heart to heart, Love flows. It is the greatest magic.

Safe now, the Pilgrim lets go of her fear of human frailties and infractions, of wounding, abandonment, and betrayal. Fox leans his head against her chest and the blessing flies through her like the Love spell that it is. Without dread or inhibition, she lets her heart open and expand. She has found the missing half she has been yearning for. She has found herself. She has learned the lesson of Love: *Look within, for when you find Love there, you will find it everywhere.* Fox curls up to sleep, safe in the Pilgrim's lap.

Essence

Love. Recognition, self-love. Devotion, companionship. The greatest magic.

Counsel

You're ready for Love. Begin or begin again, stay or go, say "yes" or "no," there is no wrong choice. Every relationship offers a mirror to see yourself clearly and a chance to discover what Love means to you and what makes you happy. It's time to discover the unconscious patterns and projections that influence your choice of partners and the dynamics in your relationships. Are you drawn to someone because they reflect missing or wounded parts of yourself?

Self-awareness and self-acceptance awaken the magic of self-Love within you, and Love heals all wounds. The Love you feel for yourself will shine from you like a lighthouse beacon, guiding Love to you. Then you can truly Love another, and who that is will be your choice. You will be free from the limitations imposed by society, religion, or upbringing.

Magic: A Love Spell

Write a Love letter to yourself. Carve your name into a red candle. Carve a heart around it. Stand in front of a mirror. Light the candle and hold it front of you. Look into your eyes until you see how much you Love yourself. Cry if you need to. Feel the gentle power and Love of the Divine that surrounds and embraces you and resides within you. Remain in those feelings of Love. When you're ready, read your Love letter to yourself. Blow out your candle and let your breath carry your spell for Love into the world. Keep your Love letter someplace safe.

17 (v) Wisdom Keeper

Wisdom

As the Pilgrim journeys on, somewhere a Wisdom Keeper is waiting. A sudden dip in the path, an unexpected detour, a sharp intake of breath upon the sighting of a deer, and then, as if by magic, the Wisdom Keeper appears.

The Pilgrim feels the subtle shift, feels electricity charge the Air and prick her skin, feels her breathing shorten and the beating of her heart quicken. She pauses, prays, then pulls aside a *tipi* flap and steps inside, into blackness. Quickly stepping out again, she sees her breath in the freezing Air and feels cold snow beneath her feet. She steps back inside the *lavuu* and, in the darkness, hears a woman ululating. She smells goats and hears their bells clinking. She steps outside again. It's hot and dry and there are women cooking. She sees desert all around her. Men are shouting, moving horses and camels. Everyone everywhere is getting on with life.

The Pilgrim steps back inside the *meharrem*. It's dark and musty. A stove is burning, and it smells of smoke, black tea, and leather. She steps outside again, into a thick, wet forest. Back in and the wind gusts wildly through the tent, swirling the magic that surrounds her. She hears many things on that wind—voices, animals, people moving, life moving in cycles, the wisdom inside aligning with the wisdom outside. She steps outside.

The Pilgrim has journeyed a long way to receive enlightenment. She sits before the Wisdom Keeper. A sacred bundle lies open between them, revealing the medicine within—healing plants and offerings, objects of power and tokens of revelation. They are spread out upon the ground, each one a part of the mystery hiding in plain sight.

Pilgrim and Wisdom Keeper sit silently together as Life goes on around them. The Pilgrim rises and departs.

A Pilgrim arrives at the Wisdom Keeper's tent. The sound of distant caribou bells is carried on the wind....

Essence

Traditional wisdom, Life, illumination. Revelations in daily existence. Spontaneous magic.

Counsel

Look at the journey you've been on. When did it begin? What were your hopes, your fears? What have you discovered about yourself? You've learned so much and yet you cannot know who you really are until you know where you are. Mother Earth is the great Wisdom Keeper and hers is the wisdom you need most now. When this card appears, it's a sign that you're ready to receive it. The blueprint of the cosmos spirals within every cell of your body—intuitive, instinctive, and certain, waiting to be seen. It awakens when you see yourself in the natural world around you. Nature is your teacher; her wisdom and her ways are encoded in your bones. Put down your phone, close your laptop, and go outside.

Magic

Place the Wisdom Keeper card before you. Study it carefully. What is your eye drawn to? What does it mean to you? Hold the deck of cards to your heart and thank it for being your oracle. Ask the deck and the Wisdom Keeper: "What do I need to know?" That's all—don't ask about love or work, money or your future. Shuffle the cards, focusing simply on what you need to know. When you're ready, pull one card. Study the image carefully, read the text, and study the image again. Reflect on what the Wisdom Keeper has shown you. Write about it. Act upon the wisdom you have been given.

18 (IV) Guardian

Wisdom

The Pilgrim's quest has stripped away fears and falsehoods. Unmade and made again by nurturing darkness and engendering light, he sees himself reflected and affirmed by the world that strengthens and sustains him. He is finding confidence and comfort far greater than wealth or privilege can provide. He has learned that there's always reason for hope. The world he lives in is sacred.

He strides forward on the path less traveled, hearing the song of Creation calling him to something greater than himself, calling him to serve. It's dawn. Mist is rising from the verdant greenwood, and because the Pilgrim is ready, the Guardian appears.

Chosen by the Goddess Sovereignty, long ago he was called the King, a title and identity sought ever since by frauds who lust for power and treasure and fakers without wisdom or humility. It's an office destined to be held by he who serves the land and all its peoples. This is what makes him worthy: holding his purpose with integrity.

Compassion, inspiration, and example are how he wields his authority, but to defend the Life he serves, he can also wield a sword against those who are cruel, indifferent, and corrupt. His wisdom and motivation arise from the order of Creation. He is the faithful and passionate partner, embodied and divine, of the Goddess, whom he has loved since the beginning of time.

His every action serves Her creed: *That all things make the world a better place for Life.*

The Pilgrim stands before the Guardian and feels the strength and gentleness that radiate from him in equal measure. A modest portion falls upon him like an honor to be carried: to till the fields and tend the animals, stand guard, and step forward. The Pilgrim is ready to be mentored and empowered by responsibility.

Essence

God. Confidence, self-respect, responsibility, integrity. Harmony, hope. Protect.

Counsel

You're coming into a true sense of yourself and your ability to create the life you want. When you're fully present and act with integrity, you'll be increasingly freed from the limitations of ego, jealousy, and selfish ambition, whether yours or someone else's. You're discovering your self-worth and earning your own respect. You're ready to serve something greater than yourself, to stand up for your values, for others, and for the wellbeing of Creation. The Guardian reminds you to seek the mentorship of the older men in your life, especially those who have offered some part of their lives in service. They will remind you what true strength is and that there's always reason for hope.

Magic

Go outside and pay attention to the trees. When you feel one calling to you, address it as the Guardian:

Guardian, power of all things
that grow, teach me how to grow,
to be strong, to serve the Life that
is greater than my own.

Sit with your back against the tree's trunk. Feel the Earth below you, the Sun above, the power of Life making all things grow. Feel it moving through you. Feel yourself growing stronger, healthier, more joyful. Remember all the good things you're creating in your life. Ask for guidance. Listen to what the Guardian has to teach you. Thank the Guardian, the tree, the grass beneath you, the Plant and Animal People around you, Mother Earth. Sense their acknowledgment. Leave an offering and act on the advice the Guardian has given you.

19 (III) Great Mother

Wisdom

In the beginning, the Great Mother poured Her starry milk across the night sky to nourish the awakening Spirits of Her children. She felt their longing to be held and loved. So powerful was the Love She felt that She began to dance, spinning faster and faster until the power of Her dancing created time and space, stars and planets, and all the elements of Creation. Her Love created the Earth, which was so beautiful that She descended to it, leaving a trail of Stars behind Her, forever circling the northernmost point in the heavens above.

Tired from Her effort, She slept, and as She slept, Love shaped Her heart and set it beating, powerful muscles covered strong bones, and thick fur kept Her Spirit warm. Air filled Her lungs, and Her womb held the Water in which Her dreams of Life took form. The Sun came closer to see the magic, and Great Mother Bear awoke to discover what Her Love had created: Her children nursing, growing, playing in a verdant landscape of abundant perfection.

In the beginning, humans called Her Artemis and thousands of other names—Queen of Heaven, Mother Earth, Womb of Creation, Oldest of the Old, Goddess from Whom All Becoming Arose and Blessings Flowed. Stars and sistrum, snakes and caves, wombs and roses—in the beginning, we knew that God was a woman. A *wicce* remembers it still.

The Pilgrim has taken her own path deep within and back again, and it has led her home. All about her, the dance of Life proceeds as everything grows a thousand-fold from a single seed. She closes her eyes and inhales deeply. Divinity has always been just a breath away.

Her eyes fly open. The Mother is seated before her, surrounded by Her Creation—nurtured, loved, provided for.

"What do you need?" The Pilgrim asks her Mother.

In that selfless moment, her own magic takes form and she knows the answer: "Love. Love your Mother, take care of Her and Her other children." She sees the Great Mother's Love poured out upon the Earth, sees its beauty and abundance and understands its wisdom: *Live and in living make the world better for all Life.*

The Pilgrim places her palms upon the ground and receives her Mother's blessing.

Essence

Goddess. Divine embodiment. Creation. Love. Nature, nurture, abundance, generosity. Blessings, fulfillment. Affirmation.

Counsel

You're perfect just the way you are. You have things to learn, skills to develop, self-acceptance and healing to attend to, but great oaks from little acorns grow. The blueprint for your soul's fulfillment and for your destiny is already within you. Mother yourself, give yourself the love and encouragement, care and reassurance, nourishment and attention you deserve. Remember, you're a child of Mother Earth.

Spend time with her. Connected to her, you're connected to yourself in all of your wholeness and mystery, tenderness and ferocity, wildness and willingness. And you're always supported, nourished, and protected by the unconditional Love from which you were created.

Magic

Create an altar for the Great Mother with natural beauty, the gifts of the season and the elements, and statues and renderings of Mother Goddesses. Create an offering to Her that expresses your love and gratitude. Take a moment every day for six weeks to honor Her at Her altar. You may wish to chant:

She changes everything She touches
and everything She touches changes.

20 (II) Priestess

Wisdom

As the Sun sets and the Moon rises, the Pilgrim climbs into the branches of the World Tree to sleep. She dreams of signs and synchronicities, messages and marvels that arrive like birds of paradise with fruits and seeds to feed her soul. A soft breeze wakens her and she remembers that the energy of Creation has flowed into her. But what is she to do with it? How is she to hold and shape it in the world? Who will teach her to make magic?

A silver cord tugs at her heart. Summoned by an ancient oracle, down the Tree's trunk she travels, down through its roots, deep down into the ground, into the Sibyl's cave. The smoke of burning bay leaves and myrrh curls about her, making the magic of sight and prophecy.

"Know yourself," she hears, and through the smoke a *Sheela na Gig* appears, the passageway of all becoming, through which comes a woman as beautiful and dark as a moonless night. One hand rests upon her heart, the other holds a wand. Cowrie shells, symbols of her station and creed, encircle her wrist and rattle as she drums a rhythm on the Moon to awaken the magic in the Pilgrim's blood.

Astride the surging Waters of Life, one foot in this world, one foot in the other, the Priestess gazes beyond space and time, into the past and the future, and into the hearts of all who seek her. She is a wise one, a traveler between worlds who knows the worlds are One. Seer of the Sacred, she dispenses holy prophecy, distributes equally wheat and fish and honey, midwives Spirits being born and departing, heals bodies, and retrieves lost souls. She speaks with plants and animals, Spirits and guides, works with wind and flame and wave and land, knows the teachings of the seasons and each seeker's destiny. She is the Priestess of every Goddess. She knows what magic is and how to make it.

Around her now, countless others are sitting in a circle, drumming the enchantment of regeneration, of their own return, and of the rebirth of Creation.

Ready now, the Pilgrim takes hold of her magic. It is time to make the world anew.

Essence

Women's mysteries. Mysteries in between. Self-knowledge. Magic and manifestation. Wisdom, prophecy, destiny. Spiritual leadership. Sacred sight.

Counsel

When you encounter the Priestess, she will ask you: "What do you want to know?" Think carefully about your answer. What do you really *need* to know to create the future that you long for? The Priestess points to your heart. The answer you're seeking is already within. Honor all that's brought you to this moment of self-awareness with love, compassion, and acceptance. The future is unfolding like a red rose blooming in the moonlight. Your magic is returning.

Magic

If you are a menstruating woman, it's time to learn your Mysteries. Pay attention to the timing of the Moon's cycle and yours, and to your feelings, intuitions, and dreams. Regardless of your gender identity, at the next full Moon, fill a bowl with Water and go outside. Hold the bowl so you can see the Moon in the Water. Look up at the Moon and call to her, then look into her mirror. Take your time. When you're ready, thank the Moon. Let any excess energy you feel flow into the Water. Leave it out overnight to charge, and in the morning pour it into a jar to use in your magic.

21 (I) Council of All Beings

Wisdom

Makers of magic have always met where Air, Fire, Water, and Earth intersect. This was the world of our Ancestors, a world of enchantment, harmony, and family. Grandmothers had wings and brothers leaves, aunts had fur, cousins fins, and the Earth was our Mother, but that was a long time ago. Led by those in love with power, so many have forgotten the power of Love.

But some still know its wonder and wisdom. They honor the blessings that flow into each of us, that fill and fulfill us, then flow from us into the world. The wise ones and Witches, the *wicces* and shamans, medicine women and cunning men, the healers and elders, *voelva*, *udagan*, *vitke*, *bruja*, *strega*, *fugara*, *mudang*, *angakok*, *bablawo*, *p'aqo*, *taltos*, and *sangoma* are bringing sacred Fires from the Earth's four corners. They know the magic of Creation. They know that Spirit and Earth are One.

They know the divine blueprint of Life is now threatened. All beings are called to Council. The Pilgrim, too, is being called.

The Animal People begin to appear. Winged beings arrive upon the wind, beings of fin burst forth from the waves and creatures of hoof, horn, and fur emerge from the forest and cross vast lands. Animals are coming from all directions. Plant People arise from the ground. The green ones are coming. The Ancestors and compassionate beings of Spirit are coming.

The Council of All Beings gathers, speaking softly to one another, laughing together, grateful for one another. The Pilgrim is welcomed into their company, into the community of Life. She is in the presence of kindness that flows to and from her open heart. She is in the presence of Spirit embodied by Creation. The Pilgrim has arrived home.

It is time to make her life the prayer.

Essence

Urgency. Summoning. Connection, community. Maturity, readiness, reverence. Kindness.

Counsel

The first thing magic changes is you. It's time to attend to the magic within and around you. Pay attention to signs and synchronicities, because they reveal the emerging pattern of your destiny. Realms of Spirit are open to you and there are guides and allies who will help you. The teachers you are seeking know that magic isn't made with supernatural or willful manipulation of unseen forces. You won't find it in someone else's incantations or recipes. Open your heart and discover what real magic is: *the power of divine Love flowing into you and through you into the world*. The Council advises that the future depends on your ability to cultivate that Love—with yourself, with Mother Earth, and all her Peoples.

Magic

Create a circle, preferably outdoors, honoring the four directions, the Sun above, Earth below, and your heart in the center. Invite the Plant and Animal Peoples, your Ancestors, and the compassionate beings of Spirit to be with you. Observe the divine wisdom embodied by Nature. What is being shown to you? Pay attention to the divinity you embody. What values do you live by? Commit to acting in accord. Offer thanks and close your circle.

0 (0) Pilgrim

Wisdom

Light of heart with dancing feet and clear eyes, the Pilgrim sets forth, knowing that every path is open before her. Beside her travels Fox, with keen senses and keener instincts, her companion and guide to the magic at play within the seeming randomness of daily events and encounters.

Patterns will emerge to reveal the Pilgrim's purpose and the meaning of her life, but it's trust rather than foresight that guides her—trust that she will be taken care of as she travels. Like a child remembering the words to the beginning of a fairy tale, she wonders where it will all lead, but everything that surrounds her is alive, connected, bountiful, and benevolent. All she has to do is recognize that.

Free from the weight or the constraints of the past, free from fear or expectations of the future, the Pilgrim is fully present in the moment, in the world, in herself. The feather in her cap reflects the enlightenment she has earned and that she seeks as her journey continues. A pentacle of apple seeds hangs above her heart, symbolizing the elements and Spirit that she, like Mother Earth, embodies. Within each seed resides magic, including the great power of rebirth. That power resides within the Pilgrim too—the power to rise again after every ending, loss, or sorrow.

The Pilgrim's journey of unmaking empowers her to make herself again, and teaches her that though the forms of Life change, the Spirit of Life is eternal. The heavens above are filled with starry paths that mirror those below. The Pilgrim walks supported, sustained, and nourished by the Love from which she was created. Mother Earth fills her path with blossoming flowers, beauty, and blessings. She walks embraced, inspired, and guided. Magic flows from Creation into her and from her into Creation.

The Pilgrim walks. Life is simple.

Essence

Awaken. Begin. Benevolence, support. Discover. Remember, trust. Continue on. Heroine's quest.

Counsel

Awaken to the magic within and around you. Weave your physical and spiritual life together, supported by the deep wisdom and love of Mother Earth. Make your life a prayer.

Magic

Cut an apple in half by slicing down its equator (across the middle, not from stem to base). Inside you will see a sacred symbol of Witches, a mystery filled with magic. Take a bite of the apple. Taste its sweetness and be mindful of and grateful for the natural abundance, generosity, love, and wisdom that support you. Make a vow to honor the blessings that you are given and to use them well for yourself and for Life. Share the rest of the apple with the animals that share your world. *So mote it be!*

Major Arcana Card Order

The following table shows the order of Major Arcana cards in the Rider Tarot and how they correspond to the Major Arcana cards of *The Witches' Wisdom Tarot.*

Rider Tarot	Rider Tarot (reversed)	Witches' Wisdom Tarot
0 The Fool	XXI World	1 World
I Magician	XX Judgment	2 Initiation
II High Priestess	XIX Sun	3 Sun
III Empress	XVIII Moon	4 Moon

Rider Tarot	Rider Tarot (reversed)	Witches' Wisdom Tarot
IV Emperor	XVII Star	5 Star
V Hierophant	XVI Tower	6 Maze
VI Lovers	XV Devil	7 Ancestor
VII Chariot	XIV Temperance	8 Healing
VIII Strength	XIII Death	9 Rebirth
IX Hermit	XII Hanged Man	10 Offering
X Wheel of Fortune	XI Justice	11 Balance
XI Justice	X Wheel of Fortune	12 Wheel of Life
XII Hanged Man	IX Hermit	13 Shaman
XIII Death	VIII Strength	14 Strength

Rider Tarot	Rider Tarot (reversed)	Witches' Wisdom Tarot
XIV Temperance	VII Chariot	15 Journey
XV The Devil	VI Lovers	16 Love
XVI The Tower	V Hierophant	17 Wisdom Keeper
XVII The Star	IV Emperor	18 Guardian
XVIII The Moon	III Empress	19 Great Mother
XIX The Sun	II High Priestess	20 Priestess
XX Judgment	I Magician	21 Council of All Beings
XXI World	0 Fool	0 Pilgrim

Keep Learning

To deepen your experiences working with the Witches' Wisdom Tarot, learn more about our work, schedule a private reading with Phyllis, or purchase Danielle's art, reach us at:

The Deck

- witcheswisdomtarot.com
- witcheswisdomtarot

Phyllis Curott

- phylliscurott.com
- Phyllis Curott
- @Phyllis Curott
- PhyllisCurottWitchcrafting

To take Phyllis's Witches' Wisdom Tarot online classes:
https://www.phylliscurott.com/shop/p/introduction-to-the-witches-wisdom-tarot-a-class-mm5sl-dfwm4-7d8ef

Danielle Barlow

daniellebarlowart.com
dbarlowart@aol.com
Danielle-Barlow-Art
@daniellebarlowart

The Green Wheel Oracle:
daniellebarlowart.com/green-wheel-oracle

To purchase Danielle's artwork:
etsy.com/shop/daniellebarlowart

About the Artist

Danielle Barlow is a painter, illustrator, and incense maker, and for the past 20 years has been a practicing Hedgewitch on the moors of Dartmoor, in the southwest of England. As well as being the co-creator of The Witches' Wisdom Tarot, she is the creator of *The Green Wheel Oracle*, and has works in collections around the world. A very busy mother of three and caretaker of animals and land, she also designs book covers and has written and illustrated for magazines.

Born in 1974, Danielle trained in textiles, then horticulture, before returning to her first love, painting. Today, she works primarily in ink and watercolor, while also stitching and practicing herbalism. Her work is deeply rooted in the ancient landscape in which she resides, exploring the physical and spiritual connections between people and the land they inhabit and drawing upon folklore and mythology. This Spirit of the land is heartfelt in her depictions of the shifting relationships between humans, animals, plants, and land. Above all, her paintings attempt to capture the elusive *genius loci*—Spirit of place.

About the Author

Phyllis Curott is a spiritual pioneer. One of America's first public Witches, she was the first to merge contemporary Witchcraft with core shamanism, rediscovering realms of spirit and the deep spiritual wisdom of Mother Earth and creating the Tradition of Ara. Phyllis is also an attorney whose groundbreaking cases secured the rights of Witches, and she is the world's most widely published Wiccan author whose internationally best-selling books have made Witchcraft accessible to the world. Her newest books include *Wicca Made Easy* and *Spells for Living Well: A Witch's Guide for Manifesting Change, Well-being, and Wonder* (Hay House UK).

Phyllis is the recipient of numerous honors, including induction into the Martin Luther King Jr. Collegium of Clergy and Scholars, *Jane* magazine's Ten Gutsiest Women of the Year Award, and One Spirit Seminary's Service to Humanity Award. Her YouTube series *What is Wicca?* has over 3 million views and her monthly Patreon Witches' Wisdom circle is attended online by folks from all over the world.

Phyllis is the Wiccan Trustee and Program Chair of the Parliament of the World's Religions, and she serves on the Advisory Board of Cherry Hill Seminary. She speaks and teaches internationally and online.

We hope you enjoyed this Hay House card deck.
If you'd like to receive additional information on
Hay House books and products, please contact:

Hay House UK, Ltd., The Sixth Floor, Watson House,
54 Baker Street, London W1U 7BU
Phone: +44 (0)20 3927 7290 • www.hayhouse.co.uk

—

Published in the United States of America by:
Hay House, Inc., P.O. Box 5100, Carlsbad,
CA 92018-5100
(760) 431-7695 or (800) 654-5126
www.hayhouse.com® • www.hayfoundation.org

—

Published in Australia by:
Hay House Australia Pty. Ltd., 18/36 Ralph St.,
Alexandria NSW 2015
Phone: 612-9669-4299 • www.hayhouse.com.au

—

Published in India by:
Hay House Publishers India, Muskaan Complex,
Plot No. 3, B-2, Vasant Kunj, New Delhi 110 070
Phone: 91-11-4176-1620 • www.hayhouse.co.in

—